YOUR recipe could appear in our next cookbook!

Share your tried & true family favorites with us instantly at
www.gooseberrypatch.com

If you'd rather jot 'em down by hand, just mail this form to...
Gooseberry Patch • Cookbooks – Call for Recipes
PO Box 812 • Columbus, OH 43216-0812

If your recipe is selected for a book, you'll receive a FREE copy!

Please share only your original recipes or those that you have made your own over the years.

Recipe Name:

Number of Servings:

Any fond memories about this recipe? Special touches you like to add
or handy shortcuts?

Ingredients (include specific measurements):

Instructions (continue on back if needed):

Special Code: **cookbookspage**

Over ➤

Extra space for recipe if needed:

Tell us about yourself...

Your complete contact information is needed so that we can send you your FREE cookbook, if your recipe is published. Phone numbers and email addresses are kept private and will only be used if we have questions about your recipe.

Name:

Address:

City: State: Zip:

Email:

Daytime Phone:

Thank you! Vickie & Jo Ann

Gooseberry Patch

Cozy Christmas COMFORTS

Tried & true recipes to make your holidays special!

Gooseberry Patch

An imprint of Globe Pequot
246 Goose Lane
Guilford, CT 06437

www.gooseberrypatch.com

1•800•854•6673

Copyright 2019, Gooseberry Patch 978-1-62093-330-5

Do you have a tried & true recipe...

tip, craft or memory that you'd like to see featured in
a **Gooseberry Patch** cookbook? Visit our website at
www.gooseberrypatch.com and follow the
easy steps to submit your favorite family recipe.
Or send them to us at:

Gooseberry Patch
PO Box 812
Columbus, OH 43216-0812

Don't forget to include the number of servings your recipe makes,
plus your name, address, phone number and email address. If we
select your recipe, your name will appear right along with it...
and you'll receive a **FREE** copy of the book!

Contents

Dedication

To everyone who loves baking cookies, choosing the perfect Christmas tree and sharing all the comfort foods of the season with family & friends...this book is for you.

Appreciation

To all of you who shared your most cherished family recipes and traditions of the holidays, a big thanks and a merry Christmas!

Sweet
Christmas
Memories

Cozy Christmas
COMFORTS

Good Friends & Good Times

Bethi Hendrickson
Danville, PA

Some of my most cherished Christmas memories were not gifts of money, but of friendship. Living on a country road in rural Pennsylvania, our neighbors were never taken for granted as we relied on each other during the good and bad times. We were blessed to have a wonderful family who lived just down the road, and we traveled back and forth often on that road from one house to the other. Christmas Day was always a blur of excitement and company. After the morning milking, Daddy would get back to the house in time for us to open the packages under the tree from Santa. Then we got dressed, the ham would be put in the oven and preparations made for family to arrive for the holiday dinner. After dinner, there was visiting, laughing and napping. After the milking was done, then the real fun for all of the kids started. Our neighbors would arrive around 7 p.m. with their four children, bringing leftovers from their Christmas dinner. Mom and Thelma would put out a huge spread of all kinds of delicious fare for us all to dine on. The new games we all received would be opened and the laughter would begin. Santa always brought a few new 45's or LP's, and I can still hear those hit songs from the 70s playing in the background. Late in the day, it was time to pack everything up and say goodbye for the day. Years later, at Christmas I still get that warm feeling of true friendship. I will forever be thankful for the lessons we learned from those simpler times and those neighbors.

Sweet Christmas Memories

Waiting for Christmas

Melissa Bromen
Marshall, MN

In the weeks leading up to Christmas every year, Mom would keep the wrapped gifts in a storeroom in our basement. No one was allowed in, which only added to the mystery and excitement! On Christmas Eve, after the "little kids" were in bed, the oldest of the six of us children were allowed to help bring up the gifts and put them under the tree. With such a large family, the number of packages seemed unbelievable as we made trip after trip with our arms full! On Christmas morning, we all gathered at the top of the stairs to wait until we were told to go down to the living room. Sometimes one of us would try to get a peek into the room, but the sliding door to the living room was closed, and the mischievous one would hear "Get back here!" and "You can't go down there!" hissed by their siblings. Finally, the door would open and Mom would say those words we were waiting to hear. Down the stairs we flew, into the magic of Christmas morning, the tree's lights shining in the early morning, and evidence that Santa had, indeed, been there!

Toy Soldier Tradition

Pat Perkins
Shenandoah, IA

When my boys were young, someone put a toy soldier in our Christmas tree. No one has ever said who did it! As my boys grew up and I had four granddaughters of my own, they helped me decorate the tree. Once the toy soldier was discovered, we had to take turns every year on who got to hide the soldier. I told my granddaughters he had guarded our tree ever year since their fathers had put the soldier in the tree. The girls have grown now and have their own trees and yes, they have a toy soldier that goes in the tree every year. I just had to buy one for each of them, as it has been so much of the fun decorating the tree every year.

Cozy Christmas
COMFORTS

The Nativity Dog

Deborah Proctor
Newborn, GA

I have a collection of Nativity sets that my granddaughter Sarah started noticing at an early age. When she was two, I decided to purchase one just for her, so that she could play with it and understand the meaning of the birth of Jesus. When the package arrived, Sarah was so excited to see what was inside the box. It was a very colorful "Little People Nativity Set." She proudly arranged it on a table in my family room. For hours, she would play with the figures and talk to them as she played. Then one day I noticed something different about her Nativity set! She had added a new animal, a small Dalmatian dog figure that belonged to her papa. I asked her why she had added the dog. Sarah told me that Max (our own Dalmatian dog) always watched over her every time she went outside, and since Baby Jesus was outside when he was born, she wanted a dog to watch over him too! So every year when she puts out her Nativity set she always includes the little Dalmatian dog figurine to keep watch over Baby Jesus.

A New Ornament Every Christmas

Doreen Knapp
Stanfordville, NY

My mother used to buy me a new Christmas ornament every Christmas. I always loved looking at them through the years. The very first Christmas ornament, the second one... My mom passed away in 1995 when I was 28, so that means she bought me 28 ornaments through the years. I still cherish every ornament that I put on my tree. I started the tradition with my own two boys. How I wish she was here to see all of my ornaments on my tree along with my sons' ornaments. It's bittersweet now, decorating our tree, but I'm so thankful that she did that. Some day my kids will know how I feel every Christmas... blessed and loved.

Sweet Christmas Memories

Christmas Memories in the 1930s   *Truda Blaylock*
Mullens, WV

I feel every Christmas is special. Gifts or no gifts, there is just something about Christmas, especially when you're a kid. When I was a little girl, we used to count down the days until Christmas. I was in Christmas programs at church and my favorite carol was "Silent Night." My brother and cousin would go out and find us a live Christmas tree, then Mom would put the tree in an old coal bucket for us to decorate. We didn't have any storebought ornaments, as far as I can recall. However, we would color sheets of paper, cut them into strips and make a colorful chain for our tree. Mom made paste for the strips by mixing flour and water. I loved our Christmas tree, and waking up Christmas morning to candy, nuts, apples, and oranges. Ever since I was small, I have always thought Christmas and anything to do with Christmas was great!

Christmas Eve in Church   *Judy Scherer*
Benton, MO

Growing up with my two sisters, every year we went to church as a family and watched my cousins in the Christmas program. At the end of the service, all the older people would get a candle, then they would light the candles, turn the lights out in church and the bright star would shine down. And then the candles were blown out. As everyone left the church, we younger kids who hadn't gotten a candle were given a sack of fruit and a candy cane. I remember wishing I could get a candle...but then when I was old enough to get a candle, I wished I could still have a sack of fruit and a candy cane again!

Cozy Christmas COMFORTS

Christmas Eve Concerts

Shirley Howie
Foxboro, MA

My older sister Joyce and I shared a love of music when we were young. Joyce played the violin and I played the piano. Around Thanksgiving time, we would start practicing Christmas carols together in preparation for the little Christmas concert we put on each year. We would wait until Mom and Dad were out of the house before we began...we wanted everything to be a surprise. We worked hard at it and wanted it to be the best it could be! We even typed up little programs to hand out to everyone, complete with our very own holiday artwork! We included the words to the carols so everyone could sing along. Aunts and uncles, cousins and grandparents all gathered to hear our little concert which we took so much pride in producing. One year I memorized the complete poem, "'Twas the Night Before Christmas" and recited it as the finale to our concert. Everyone loved it! I often think about those magical Christmas Eves so long ago when we were all gathered together and the joy we brought to those we loved.

Decorating the Christmas Tree

Ann Viviano
Saint John, IN

Christmas is my favorite time of year. In my mind's eye, I can go back to my childhood and recall memories of the days leading up to Christmas. Christmas carols playing on the record player while my father put the lights on our evergreen tree with such perfection. My mother decked out in her red & white checked apron, baking every kind of cookie you could dream of. And my dog Trixie, sitting and patiently wagging her tail, waiting for me to share a taste of one of those wonderful treats with her. These memories are still sweet.

Sweet Christmas Memories

Thirty Years of Christmas Cookies
Karen Burger
Hagerstown, MD

In 1988 when I was five, my mom was pregnant with my sister and was on bed rest. That year, my dad and I baked the cookies together. I think cookie baking with my dad was meant more as a distraction for both of us, but it spawned a tradition that has lasted for 30 years. Every single Christmas, except for one when I was living outside the country, Dad and I have spent at least two days baking hundreds of cookies. We make everything from chocolate no-bake to malted milk to good old-fashioned gingerbread with candy hearts. Originally we gave them to our church choir where my dad directed and to my school bus driver and teachers. Now we give them to co-workers and extended family & friends all over the country. Everyone, from cousins to co-workers to friends old and new, anticipates our cookie baking days. Now my young son joins the fun as well, mostly as a taster!

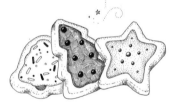

There's No Place Like Home
Sheila Galus
Mantua, OH

We moved from New York state to Ohio in 1972. I was seven, my brother was nine. It broke our hearts because we were leaving our family & friends behind. Every Christmas we'd go back home. My grandparents didn't have much money, but they would scrimp and save all year for that one special day. On Christmas morning, we woke up to the aroma of turkey roasting in the oven, carols playing on the radio and my grandparents sitting by the tree waiting to pass out the gifts from Santa. Aunts and uncles, cousins and friends all crowded around that old dining room table. We'd tell stories of Christmases past, of relatives who we missed and how much we have to be thankful for. Those days are gone, but every year, especially at Christmastime, I always think about all the love and laughter we shared every time we went home for Christmas.

Cozy Christmas
COMFORTS

Creating New Christmas Memories

Shannon James
Georgetown, KY

My childhood was filled with classic Christmas traditions... laughing as we decorated sugar cookies, rushing downstairs on Christmas morning and having our large family over for Christmas dinner. I try to create similar memories for our four children. Unfortunately, we live far away from both sides of our families. The traditions and excitement of Christmas morning are still rampant in our home, but afterwards, it is difficult knowing that we are not going to see family for Christmas dinner. Instead we began a new tradition. After the presents have been unwrapped and phone calls made to family, the six of us pack our bags and head to a local hotel that is known for its amazing Christmas decorations, gigantic Christmas trees, "snow" in the lobby and an indoor water park. The hotel also serves an amazing Christmas dinner. I know it is not the same as spending time with extended family, but the six of us have a beautiful day filled with family, food and fun. Now we are making new memories together and we all look forward to Christmas morning.

Over the river and through the wood,
To grandmother's house we go...
– Lydia Maria Child

Sweet Christmas *Memories*

The Priceless Tree

Narita Roady
Pryor, OK

One Christmas when we were expecting our third child, money was
tight. We decided to head to the country in our small car and cut down
a scrub pine. Driving down the road, we spotted a beautiful huge tree.
We had to tilt our heads back to see the top! It was way too big for our
house, so my husband topped it off as far as he would reach. With
much maneuvering, we got it into our hatchback car with it sticking far
out the back. Once home, we had to trim even more even due to the
12-foot ceiling in our den. When we put it on our tree stand, the metal
literally folded and bent, so that meant a quick trip to the store for a
sturdy new stand. Once up, we found our decorations, lights and
garland covered only a third of it! Another trip to the store...so much
for saving money! Finally it was up and it was incredible. We couldn't
wait for our parents to see it. Mother walked in the door and said,
"I can't believe it! Some fool cut the top out of a huge pine that has
been there since before I was a little girl." My husband put his arm
around her and said, "Mom, come to the fool's den and see the tree."
That was the best Christmas tree we ever had!

Christmas Sock Exchange

Vickie Wiseman
Liberty Twp., OH

Several years ago, we started doing something a little different for
Christmas. We have family scattered all over, as well as locally, and it
is hard to get everyone together. We're in Ohio, while others are in
Illinois, Kansas, Tennessee, New York and even Alaska. We draw
names on or around Thanksgiving. Then we buy our person a pair of
socks that may or may not fit their personality. We fill thes socks with
small things...candy, a toy, a nutcracker or something else they would
like or be amused by. We each send the socks to our person, or bring
them to our Christmas celebration if they will be there. We agree on a
time that we can all get together on Skype, so everyone can open their
surprise-filled socks. It is hilarious watching everyone! They have to
model their socks after they put them on, and we take pictures.
Everyone enjoys this very much, and it is hilarious to see what
everyone gets. It's a great solution for a far-flung family.

Cozy Christmas COMFORTS

The Year I Found Out About Santa

Joyce Sipe
New Wilmington, PA

The Christmas of 1956, I was only five years old and was the youngest child in our family. On Christmas Eve, my older sister and brother and I decided to peek through the cold air register in my parents' bedroom, which overlooked the living room where our Christmas tree stood in the corner. I could see my father putting gifts under the tree, but I insisted to my siblings that Santa was just out of sight, handing them to Dad. To prove me wrong, we all sneaked down the stairway so we could look through the keyhole of the hallway door and get a better view of the living room. I still cannot remember who bumped the door handle with their head (my siblings claim it was me), but Dad heard and headed over to investigate. We tried to get up the stairs in time, but didn't make it. Instead of being punished, we were allowed to stay up and each open a single gift. My brother got a set of Roy Rogers cap guns. My sister opened up pajamas, oops. I opened up a beautiful doll and since I had also gotten a child-sized rocking chair which was not wrapped, I spent the extra time rocking my doll while sitting in my rocking chair. It is one of my favorite memories of Christmas from my childhood. And all these many years later, I still have the little rocking chair!

Happier Times at Christmas

Leona Vinca
Eminence, KY

When my children were very young, my husband and I were out of work. So the five of us drew names and decided we would each spend one dollar on a gift for that person. On Christmas Eve we went to church. When we got back home, there were presents waiting for the children, cookies, groceries and a card with some money in it, signed only, "Your friends in Christ." It was the best Christmas ever, seeing how God cared for us and does care for us always when we trust Him, just rejoicing in His goodness.

Sweet Christmas Memories

Ornaments for the Tree

Rebecca Meadows
Hinton, WV

There are so many memories that Christmastime can bring, but my favorite is decorating the Christmas tree. For me, what's most special is the memories from the ornaments as they go up on the tree. When I was a teenager, I started to buy an ornament from each place I visited, and I have continued to do so. As I place each special, sentimental ornament on my tree, the memories and love from that trip or event in life come flooding back, making Christmas an even more magical time. Each ornament has a special meaning and the places and events they recall can be celebrated each Christmas and many more to come.

Our Christmas Tree

Tyleen Miller
New Ulm, MN

I remember every Christmas as a child, our tree was always a real tree. And it looked so full and beautiful and smelled wonderful! My mom always made sure it was full of twinkling lights and all of our old ornaments. It didn't make any difference that they were the same ones each year, I loved them. My sisters and I would play "guess the ornament." There were so many that it was hard to find the right one... but with time, we did! I also loved to lie under the tree when it was lit and just gaze up through the branches. It was so pretty. Now I have an artificial tree for convenience, but there's still nothing to compare to my mom and her beautiful real Christmas tree.

Cozy Christmas
COMFORTS

O Christmas Tree,
O Christmas Tree

Cyndi Little
Whitsett, NC

We had recently moved into our new house and I was determined to have my "live" Christmas tree the day after Thanksgiving. I asked my husband about going to get a tree, only to receive his standard "um-hum" which means...that's not going to happen. By this time, I had decided that not only would I go and buy my Christmas tree myself, I would drive to the mountains to get a tree. I called my sister-in-law to see if she wanted to ride with me to get a tree. Bright and early Friday morning, she and I pulled out. My trusty van's gas tank was filled and Christmas music blasted from the cassette player. Lots of chatter, laughter and hot coffee later, we arrived in the foothills of the mountains and decided that was close enough to say we'd gone to the mountains. I found a tree lot that was selling all trees for $20 each. Thinking I probably wouldn't find "the" tree, I pulled in. We got out of the van and began to search. Yes! There it was! Not only was it "the" tree, it was more than I required to be the perfect tree. Three feet more, to be exact! I asked if the tree could be tied to the top of the van, only to be told, not unless I had brought twine or rope, which of course, I had not. So, I decided that tree could ride inside the van. Both my sister-in-law and the tree lot owner told me it wouldn't fit, after all, it was at least ten feet tall. But I was determined that it would and could not be talked out of trying. So with much pushing, pulling and shoving, that ten-foot tree went into my van...all the way to the front, with the very tip-top resting on the dash! We managed to close the back hatch, and with lots of laughter and calls of "Good luck!" we were on our way home. Yes, I did get the perfect tree. Yes, I did have to have three feet trimmed off of the tree...and, yes, unfortunately, my husband got to say "I told you so" when that same tree was brown and dry as a bone within two weeks and had to be replaced. Lesson learned? Not on your life! I still want my live tree the Friday after Thanksgiving! Every year we have the same discussion, always beginning with,"Do you remember the year...?" So many funny memories!

16

Sweet Christmas *Memories*

Childhood Christmas

Stephanie O'Connor
Ontario, Canada

Christmas was always my favorite holiday. Even as a child, it wasn't just the gifts and the treats that made it special. It was our tradition in our family to stay up on Christmas Eve and go to a candlelit midnight church service. We got to dress up even more fancy than usual for church, and often got a new dress just for the occasion. The next day, we would do our usual Christmas gift opening, but it was Christmas Eve that was the most special. We would all go to my grandma's and have a feast. She would be cooking for days in advance, and it would all be served on her fine china...even we kids were allowed to eat off it! Then we would all relax with dessert and tea and slowly open our gifts to each other. To this day, when I see my kids opening their gifts, eating their Christmas dinner, it brings back those warm memories of my childhood. And I always pray that they reflect and are thankful when they are grown and celebrating with their own babies.

Girls' Night Christmas

Donna Carter
Ontario, Canada

My special Christmas memory comes every year around the second week of December. My longtime friend Trudy always hosts a Girls' Night at her home and includes just a few special friends...myself, another Donna and Barb. We have been getting together for well over ten years now, just a cozy night of hot tea, food and lots of talking and laughter. Oh, and gifts too! We don't always see each other often during the year, but Girls' Night Christmas is a must.

Cozy Christmas
COMFORTS

Family Christmases

Barbara Klein
Newburgh, IN

My parents were married in 1946. Now at 71, I am the oldest of seven siblings, and my youngest sibling is 50. Quite an age spread, and what a variety of personalities! My father and mother loved the Thanksgiving and Christmas holidays with family. We always hosted family at our table at both Thanksgiving and Christmas. As the years went by, the group became quite large. At one holiday, I counted 65 people in my parents' home! On Christmas Day, after eating a sumptuous meal, we would all gather around the piano. Along with other musical instruments playing and voices raised, the musicality of our family rocked! My dad was a great tenor and we all sang the songs of the season together in harmony. My sister played the piano, my daughter played the keyboard, my brother and nephews played guitars, my niece played the violin and the rest joined in song. What great memories! When the grandkids came along, we included them in many of their favorites. One favorite, "The Twelve Days of Christmas," was sung with gusto as a different group sang each day of the song. Alas, my father passed away in 2009 at the age of 86. However, my mother at age 92 still hosts family holiday meals. We all chip in with the food, but the space in the house seems smaller as there are now siblings, grandkids, great-grandkids, in-laws and in some cases in-laws' families. Again in 2018, we looked forward to all being together as a family to celebrate the seasons, much to the delight of my mother and the rest of us.

Sweet Christmas *Memories*

Family Cookie Exchange

Elizabeth Smithson
Cunningham, KY

In 1962, my mom thought the girls in the family should do something special together, just for us! So we started the wonderful tradition of a cookie exchange. It began with four people and now we have grown to 20! We share brunch together, and share enough cookies for tasting and to take home. There are prizes for best-tasting cookie, best presentation and all-around best. We have a "dirty Santa" ornament exchange too. This year, for a gift, we filled pretty Christmas socks full of goodies and drew numbers for those. Our cookie exchange is always the first Saturday in December and my sweet mom is still with us at 91. I hope she is around for more fun and laughter all day! I will always remember all the memories, as we have lost a few participants, but this year we are adding two new ones. I have told the young ones they have to carry this tradition on. Fun, fun, fun!

A Handmade Christmas Tree

Dana Alexander
Lebanon, MO

Some years ago, we were planning to move in early December. We packed and boxed up everything, including all our Christmas ornaments. Moving was delayed and all we had was the tree. Being crafty, we just made our own ornaments. Everything from construction paper chains to popcorn garlands to origami shapes was hung on the tree. I didn't think much of it, and it was only recently that my daughter recounted the fun we'd had making all the decorations together. It's not the stuff you have...it's the memories!

Cozy Christmas
COMFORTS

Visions of Sugarplums

Kristy Wells
Ocala, FL

Growing up, we didn't have much, and my parents always made the best of what we had. Mom would pack us into the car to ride around town looking at all the Christmas lights in neighborhoods ready for the season. We visited a home decorated with thousands of lights, where an old couple dressed as Santa & Mrs. Claus handed out candy canes to all the good little boys and girls. Eventually we would return home. My most treasured memory is of Mom letting my baby brother and me camp out under the Christmas tree. I still remember the glow of the twinkling lights, the smell of pine and the occasional tickle of tinsel against my cheek. Such a magical time in a young child's life...truly amazing and forever treasured. I have continued these wonderful customs with my children and hope to one day pass them along to their children too.

Arkansas Christmas Memories

Beckie Apple
Grannis, AR

I have cherished Christmas memories of growing up in rural Arkansas. We lived on a country road in the community of Blue Ball, just a few hundred feet from our maternal grandparents. We kids loved spending time with Pop and Mim. Christmas at their house was such a special time for me and my brothers and sisters. Mim would have a small real tree with homemade decorations. Even now, I can almost smell the wonderful aroma coming from her kitchen. She would have roast turkey, baked stuffed duck, cornbread dressing, gravy, sweet potatoes and real mashed potatoes. Pumpkin pie and sometimes apple pie would be waiting for anyone with any room left to hold it...and we kids always had room! There was an atmosphere of Christmas there that sadly these 50 years later is really missed. I'm happy to have these memories.

Sweet Christmas *Memories*

Santa's Sleigh Bells

Pam Watson
Brooktondale, NY

For years, my husband would ring sleigh bells on Christmas Eve after our daughters were in bed. He'd stand outside the house at a distance from their bedroom and ring away. It always made them giggle, smile and snuggle under the covers to get to sleep. When they were too old for that, he began going to our youngest niece's house. One year he rang the bells, then walked away to where he had parked his car on the road. We didn't know until the next morning that one of the bells had fallen off the strap and landed in my sister's driveway. Our niece found it! Not only had she heard Santa, but she got to keep one of his bells! She is a teenager now. I wonder if she still has it?

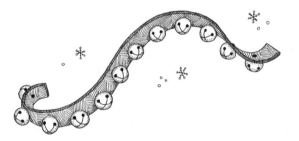

Christmas Eve Traditions

Brenda Montgomery
Lebanon, IN

When I was a kid in the 1960s, Christmas Eve was a special evening with my sister, mom and dad. A little while after dinner, Dad would take four glass bottles of Coca-Cola and bury them in the snow under the bush by the front porch steps. Then a little later, Mom popped some popcorn while my sister and I would put on our coats and boots and go out and get the bottles out of the snow. We would all watch a Christmas movie together while eating popcorn and drinking Coca-Cola. Maybe we'd even string some for the tree! We would also have an apple to eat. It was always such a special time that my sister and I looked forward to going out and getting those Cokes out of the snow.

Cozy Christmas
COMFORTS

Family Cabin Christmas Party

Mary Motte
Henderson, NV

Every December on the Saturday before Christmas, members big and small of the Haight family gather in a cabin in the woods of upstate New York for our annual family Christmas party. This was born of our ever-expanding group becoming too large to fit in anyone's home. My mom and dad, aunts and uncles started renting a cabin in the woods, complete with kitchen, to accommodate us all. We all share slow cookers of homemade soups, snacks and desserts made by three generations. Dad and his brothers bring a live tree for everyone to decorate with Great-Grandpa and Grandma's old ornaments. A pageant commemorating the birth of Christ is held in the collapsible Nativity made by Uncle Dan, topped off by a visit from Santa, sledding, singing and games. We celebrated the 26th year of our family tradition in 2018!

Christmas Eve with Santa

Debs Dudoit
Honolulu, HI

Every Christmas Eve, my grandmas, aunties, uncles, cousins, sister, brother, nieces, nephews, grand-nieces and friends have come over to my parents' home for Christmas Eve dinner. Santa Claus always comes by after dinner for Christmas carols and crafts or games. Santa passes out candy and gifts from his big red bag. He reads all the gift tags on the presents under the tree and the keiki (children) distribute them to our ohana (family). We take individual and family pictures with Santa, then we say our fond Aloha to Santa and hope to see him the next year. We are going on my 60th year of doing this and hope the tradition continues on for many more years. Mele Kalikimaka!

Holiday
Breakfast &
Brunch

Christmas Egg Casserole

Linda Franks
Lafayette, GA

When our kids were little, their grandparents liked to come over on Christmas morning to see their presents. We started having Christmas breakfast together every year and have continued to do so. This dish you make the night before and refrigerate overnight, then get up in the morning and slide into the oven. By the time presents are opened, it is ready...perfect!

3 c. seasoned croutons
15 eggs, beaten
2 c. milk
1 t. seasoned salt
1/2 t. onion powder

1-1/2 c. shredded Cheddar
   cheese
Optional: 1-1/2 c. cooked ham,
   sausage or bacon, chopped

Coat a 13"x9" baking pan with non-stick vegetable spray. Spread croutons in pan; set aside. In a large bowl, whisk together eggs, milk and seasonings. Fold in cheese and meat, if using; pour over croutons. Cover and chill for 8 hours, stirring once. Next morning, uncover casserole and stir. Bake, uncovered, at 350 degrees for 30 minutes, or until eggs are set. Makes 8 to 10 servings.

Celebrate the season with a holiday brunch buffet for friends and neighbors! It's a joyful time of year to renew old acquaintances while sharing scrumptious food together.

Holiday Breakfast & Brunch

French Toast with Honey Cranberries

Vickie
Gooseberry Patch

A scrumptious twist on an old favorite.

5 eggs, beaten
2/3 c. milk
1/4 c. sugar
1 t. vanilla extract
4 T. butter, divided

8 slices whole-grain or
   white bread
4 to 6 thin slices Brie cheese
Optional: warmed honey

Make Honey Cranberries ahead of time. In a shallow dish, whisk together eggs, milk, sugar and vanilla; set aside. Melt 2 tablespoons butter in a large non-stick skillet over medium heat. Dip 2 slices of bread into egg mixture until well coated. Add to skillet and cook for 3 to 5 minutes per side, until golden. Repeat with remaining butter and bread. Arrange French toast slices on a serving plate, alternating with slices of cheese and spoonfuls of Honey Cranberries. Serve with honey on the side, if desired. Makes 4 servings, 2 slices each.

Honey Cranberries:

2 T. butter
2 c. fresh or frozen cranberries

1/3 c. honey

Melt butter in a saucepan over medium heat; add cranberries and honey. Cook until cranberries are soft and honey has thickened, about 3 minutes.

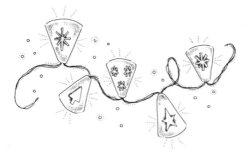

String small nutmeg graters on a set of white lights
for a sweet kitchen garland.

Cozy Christmas
COMFORTS

Vanilla Streusel Coffee Cake

Debbie Keyes
Lafayette, IN

This is our family's go-to coffee cake for Christmas morning.

3 c. all-purpose flour
1-1/2 t. baking powder
1-1/2 t. baking soda
1/4 t. salt
1-1/2 c. butter, softened
1-1/2 c. sugar
3 eggs

1-1/2 c. sour cream
1-1/2 t. vanilla extract
3/4 c. chopped nuts
3/4 c. brown sugar, packed
1-1/2 t. cinnamon
2 T. vanilla extract
2 T. water

In a bowl, sift together flour, baking powder, baking soda and salt; set aside. In a large bowl, combine butter and sugar; beat until fluffy. Add eggs, one at a time, beating well after each addition. Blend in sour cream and vanilla. Gradually add flour mixture to butter mixture; stir well. In another bowl, combine nuts, brown sugar and cinnamon. Spoon 1/3 of batter into a buttered 10" tube pan; sprinkle with 1/2 of nut mixture. Repeat layers, ending with batter. Whisk together vanilla and water in a cup; spoon over top. Bake at 325 degrees for 60 to 70 minutes. Cool completely in pan before turning out cake. Serves 12.

Nothing says Christmas like the wonderful fragrance of freshly cut evergreens! Arrange tree trimmings into vases to enjoy the aroma throughout the house.

Holiday Breakfast & Brunch

Heavenly Hotcakes

Tracie Carlson
Richardson, TX

These hotcakes originated with an old Amish recipe. I accidentally changed the recipe when I first tried it. The result...simply divine, the lightest, fluffiest pancakes! We always make the same "mistake" now.

2 c. all-purpose flour
1 t. baking powder
1-1/2 t. baking soda
1 t. salt
2 eggs, beaten

2 c. buttermilk
1/4 c. butter, melted
1 t. vanilla extract
Garnish: warm maple syrup,
    sliced fruit, jam

Sift together flour, baking powder, baking soda and salt. Add remaining ingredients except garnish. Stir lightly, just until moistened. Batter will be thick and lumpy. Lightly oil a skillet or griddle; heat over medium heat until a drop of water bounces around when dropped onto it. Drop batter onto hot griddle by 1/2 cupfuls; spread slightly with a spoon. Cook until edges of pancake look dry and small bubbles appear, about 2 minutes. Turn over and cook other side. Garnished as desired. Makes 9 large pancakes; serves 4 to 5.

Angel's Syrup

Jill Ball
Highland, UT

This is our family's favorite syrup. We are sure this is what the angels in heaven eat for breakfast! Serve hot over pancakes, waffle and crepes.

1 c. butter, sliced
1 c. buttermilk
2 c. sugar

1 t: vanilla extract
1 t. baking soda

In a large saucepan over medium heat, bring butter, buttermilk and sugar to a boil for 2 minutes. Cook and stir until sugar dissolves. Remove from heat. Stir in vanilla and baking soda; mixture will froth up. Serve hot; store in refrigerator. Serves 6.

Cozy Christmas
COMFORTS

Sausage & Spinach Egg Bake

Carolyn Deckard
Bedford, IN

Seems like we are always in a hurry! This is good for breakfast or brunch and so easy to put together. The red and green colors of the peppers and spinach make it perfect for the holidays too.

1 lb. ground Italian pork sausage
1/2 c. onion, chopped
7-oz. jar roasted red peppers, drained, chopped and divided
10-oz. pkg. frozen chopped spinach, thawed and squeezed dry
1 c. all-purpose flour
1/4 c. grated Parmesan cheese
1 t. dried basil
1/2 t. salt
8 eggs, beaten
2 c. milk
1 c. shredded provolone cheese

In a skillet over medium heat, brown sausage with onion; drain. Transfer to a greased 3-quart casserole dish. Sprinkle with half of the red peppers; top with all the spinach. In a large bowl, combine flour, Parmesan cheese and seasonings; set aside. In a separate bowl, whisk together eggs and milk; stir into flour mixture until blended. Pour over spinach. Bake, uncovered, at 425 degrees for 15 to 20 minutes, until eggs are set and a knife tip inserted near the center comes out clean. Top with provolone cheese and remaining peppers. Bake for 3 to 5 minutes longer, until cheese is melted. Let stand for 5 minutes before serving. Makes 6 servings.

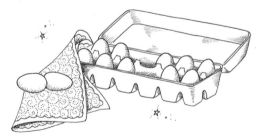

On busy holiday days, a little kitchen prep the night before is really helpful. Whisk up eggs for scrambling, stir together dry ingredients for waffles and lay out tableware ahead of time. In the morning, you'll be a relaxed hostess!

Tomato-Cheese Quiche

Eleanor Dionne
Beverly, MA

Love this...it's one of my favorites!

2 onions, finely chopped
2 T. butter
1 clove garlic, minced
14-1/2 oz. can whole tomatoes,
    sliced and juice reserved
1/4 c. fresh parsley, chopped
1/4 t. dried thyme

1/2 t. salt
1/8 t. cayenne pepper
10-inch pie crust, unbaked
2 c. shredded Swiss cheese
3 eggs, beaten
1/2 c. whole black olives,
    cut into wedges

In a large skillet over medium heat, cook onions in butter until soft and golden; stir in garlic. Add tomatoes with juice, parsley, thyme, salt and cayenne pepper. Bring to a boil; reduce heat to medium-low. Cover and simmer for 15 minutes. Remove from heat. Line a 10" quiche pan with crust; trim edges. Sprinkle cheese into crust; set aside. Beat eggs in a large bowl; gradually stir in tomato mixture. Fold in olives. Pour tomato mixture over cheese in pie crust. Set pan on lowest oven rack. Bake at 450 degrees for 10 minutes. Reduce heat to 350 degrees. Continue baking for 25 to 30 minutes, until center is set and crust is golden. Let stand about 5 minutes before cutting into wedges. Serves 6.

Tie tiny Christmas ornaments onto stemmed glasses with ribbon bows...so festive for serving orange juice at a holiday brunch.

Cozy Christmas
COMFORTS

Mom's Christmas Morning Cranberry Bread

Vivian Tapanes
Fort Myers, FL

I started making this cranberry bread on my son's first Christmas and it has been a family favorite ever since. Very simple to make, but leaves a lasting memory in your tummy. Enjoy!

2 c. all-purpose flour
1 c. sugar
1-1/2 t. baking powder
1/4 t. baking soda
1/2 t. salt
1/3 c. butter

1 egg, lightly beaten
1 t. orange zest
2/3 c. orange juice
1-1/2 c. fresh cranberries, halved
1 c. nuts, coarsely chopped

In a large bowl, stir together flour, sugar, baking powder, baking soda and salt. Cut in butter with a fork until mixture looks like coarse crumbs; set aside. In a small bowl, whisk together egg, orange zest and juice. Add to flour mixture and stir until moistened. Fold in cranberries and nuts. Spoon batter into a lightly greased 9"x5" loaf pan. Bake at 350 degrees for 60 to 70 minutes, until a toothpick inserted in center tests done. Cool loaf in pan on a wire rack for about 10 minutes. Remove from pan; cool completely. Wrap and store overnight before slicing. Makes one loaf.

A loaf of homemade fruit bread is always a welcome gift.
Make sure it stays fresh and tasty...let the bread cool completely,
then wrap well in plastic wrap or aluminum foil.

Holiday Breakfast & Brunch

Perfect Hot Cocoa Mix

Hollie Moots
Marysville, OH

When my kids were little, they loved to help measure, stir and bag up this mix as gifts for teachers and friends. Such good memories! It makes the most delicious, rich hot cocoa that people request, year after year! And it's easily doubled.

2 c. powdered milk
1/2 c. powdered non-dairy
   creamer
3/4 c. sugar

1/2 c. baking cocoa
1/2 c. mini semi-sweet
   chocolate chips
1/4 t. salt

Combine all ingredients in a bowl; whisk until well mixed. Store in a tightly covered container at room temperature. For gifts, spoon a cup of cocoa mix into a plastic zipping bag; tuck into a mug. Tie on a bow and the directions: To make hot chocolate, spoon 3 or 4 generous tablespoons of cocoa mix into a mug. Add one cup boiling water and stir well. Makes 4 cups cocoa mix.

Mocha Coffee Mix

Karen Schmidt
Racine, WI

I often give this coffee mix as a Christmas gift. It is so good!
I always get compliments and thank you's for it.

1-3/4 c. powdered milk
1-1/2 c. chocolate drink mix
6 T. instant coffee granules

1/2 c. powdered non-dairy
   creamer
2 T. powdered sugar

Combine all ingredients in a large bowl; stir until well blended. Transfer to a wide-mouth 2-quart canning jar. Attach a gift label with the directions: To make mocha coffee, spoon 4 tablespoons coffee mix into a mug; add one cup boiling water. Stir until dissolved. If desired, garnish with whipped cream and shaved chocolate. Makes 4 cups coffee mix.

Cozy Christmas
COMFORTS

Holiday French Toast Bake

Theresa Eldridge
Festus, MO

My mom showed her love through cooking. Every Christmas, she would have something delicious baking while we all opened gifts by the big fireplace in the living room. We still keep our Christmas breakfast tradition even though she has passed away...it is a great way to keep her memory with us. This casserole has become a family favorite, and I hope you love it as much as we do. I make this often!

1 loaf day-old French bread,
    cut into one-inch cubes
Optional: 1 to 2 c. fresh
    cranberries or blueberries
8 eggs, beaten
2-1/2 c. milk

1/2 c. sugar
2 T. cinnamon
2 T. vanilla extract
Optional: pancake syrup,
    or fresh fruit, honey and
    powdered sugar

Place bread cubes in a greased 13"x9" baking pan. Sprinkle with berries, if using; set aside. In a bowl, whisk together remaining ingredients except garnish. Pour over bread cubes, covering well. Cover and refrigerate for several hours or overnight. To bake, uncover pan; stir to make sure bread cubes are coated evenly. If desired, pour Optional Topping over all. Set pan on a baking sheet to catch any drips. Bake, uncovered, at 350 degrees for 40 to 50 minutes. Garnish as desired. Serves 6 to 8.

Optional Topping:

1-1/3 c. brown sugar, packed
3/4 c. butter, sliced

3 T. light corn syrup

Combine all ingredients in a saucepan over medium heat. Cook and stir until boiling and brown sugar is dissolved.

Holiday Breakfast & Brunch

Hot Fruit Casserole

Julie Dixon
Longview, TX

This recipe is from my husband's niece, Wendy. It is easy and delicious, and has become one of our family's favorites during the holidays. Easy to make ahead and reheat for serving!

20-oz. jar applesauce
21-oz. can cherry pie filling
20-oz. can pineapple tidbits, drained
15-oz. can apricot halves, drained and cut into quarters
15-oz. can sliced pears, drained and cut into bite-size pieces
15-oz. can sliced peaches, drained and cut into bite-size pieces
1-1/2 c. light brown sugar, packed
1 T. cinnamon
Optional: 1/4 to 1/2 c. sherry

Spread applesauce in an ungreased 13"x9" glass baking pan. Top with pie filling. Layer remaining fruits over pie filling; set aside. Combine brown sugar and cinnamon in a bowl; sprinkle over fruit mixture. Drizzle with sherry, if using. Bake, uncovered, at 325 degrees for one hour, until hot and bubbly. Serve warm. Makes 8 to 10 servings.

Fill a garden bell jar with clementines, pomegranates and shiny green apples. Cover the opening with a plate and turn right-side up. A centerpiece in no time at all!

Cozy Christmas
COMFORTS

Stuffed French Toast

Cinda Lasinski
Centennial, CO

I began making this recipe for my family years ago for our traditional Christmas morning brunch. It was such a huge success that I decided to make it every year. By changing the pie filling, I have a new recipe each time. It's easy to make and my grandchildren absolutely love it... the adults do too!

8 thick slices Italian bread,
  cubed and divided
2 8-oz. pkgs. reduced-fat cream
  cheese, cubed
1 to 2 21-oz. cans light cherry,
  blueberry or peach pie filling

1 doz. eggs, beaten, or equivalent
  egg substitute
2 c. skim milk
1/3 c. pure maple syrup
1/8 t. nutmeg or cinnamon

Spread half of the bread cubes in a greased 13"x9" baking pan. Scatter cream cheese cubes over bread. If using 2 cans pie filling, partially drain. Spoon pie filling evenly over cream cheese. Top with remaining bread. In a bowl, whisk together remaining ingredients; pour over bread and cheese. Cover and refrigerate overnight. Bake at 375 degrees for 45 minutes, or until hot and eggs are set. Serves 10 to 12.

Whip up a luscious topping to dollop on pancakes and waffles...yum! Combine 3/4 cup whipping cream, 2 tablespoons softened cream cheese and one tablespoon powdered sugar. Beat with an electric mixer on medium speed until soft peaks form. Keep refrigerated in a small covered crock.

Super-Duper Baked Oatmeal

Louisa Abello
Bemidji, MN

We kids like this a lot more than plain old oatmeal,
especially when some yummy toppings are added!

1/2 c. butter, melted
2 eggs, beaten
1 c. milk
1/2 c. brown sugar, packed
2 t. baking powder
1 t. vanilla extract
2 t. cinnamon

1/8 t. salt
3 c. long-cooking oats, uncooked
Optional: 1/4 c. flaked coconut,
   butterscotch chips, cinnamon
   chips, blueberries and/or
   chopped apple
Garnish: cream or milk

Spread melted butter in a 2-quart casserole dish; set aside. In a large
bowl, whisk together eggs, milk, brown sugar, baking powder, vanilla,
cinnamon and salt. Stir in oats; spoon into casserole dish. Sprinkle
with desired topping, if using. Cover with plastic wrap and refrigerate
overnight. In the morning, uncover and bake at 350 degrees for
45 minutes, or until golden and bubbling at the edges. Serve topped
with cream or milk. Makes 4 to 6 servings.

Streamline your holiday plans this year. Ask your family what
traditions they most look forward to, including favorite cookies
and other festive foods. Then you can focus on tried & true activities,
freeing up time to try something new and meaningful to you.

Cozy Christmas
COMFORTS

Spinach & Swiss Quiche

Joyceann Dreibelbis
Wooster, OH

Swiss cheese, crisp bacon and spinach mingle in a pie crust to create a delicious breakfast dish. Perfect for brunch or a light lunch too.

9-inch pie crust, unbaked
1 c. shredded Swiss cheese
4 slices bacon, crisply cooked
   and crumbled
2 T. butter
1 shallot, chopped

1 c. frozen chopped spinach,
   thawed and squeezed dry
salt and pepper to taste
Optional: 1/8 t. nutmeg
3 eggs, beaten
1-1/2 c. half-and-half

Bake pie crust according to package directions. Sprinkle cheese and bacon into baked pie crust; set aside. Melt butter in a skillet; sauté shallot and spinach for 2 to 3 minutes. Sprinkle with seasonings; remove from heat. In a bowl, beat eggs and half-and-half. Add spinach mixture; stir well and pour into pie crust. Bake at 375 degrees for 25 to 30 minutes, until a knife tip inserted near the center comes out clean. Let stand for 15 minutes; cut into wedges. Serves 6.

Vintage salt & pepper shakers, in the shape of snowmen or Mr. & Mrs. Santa, add a touch of holiday cheer to any table and a smile to guests' faces.

Holiday Breakfast & Brunch

Sausage Muffins

Josh Logan
Victoria, TX

These savory muffins are great for breakfast...even if you're on the run. Just wrap one or two in a napkin and go!

1/2 lb. ground pork breakfast
 sausage
2 c. all-purpose flour
2 T. sugar
1 T. baking powder
1/4 t. salt

1 egg, lightly beaten
1 c. milk
1/4 c. butter, melted and slightly
 cooled
1/2 c. shredded Cheddar cheese

Brown sausage in a skillet over medium heat; drain. Meanwhile, in a large bowl, combine flour, sugar, baking powder and salt; mix well and make a well in center. In a separate bowl, whisk together egg, milk and butter. Add to flour mixture and stir just until moistened. Stir in sausage and cheese. Spoon batter into 12 greased muffin cups, filling 2/3 full. Bake at 375 degrees for 20 minutes, or until golden. Immediately remove from pan. Makes one dozen.

Tomato-Bacon Tarts

Lisanne Miller
Wells, ME

Great little breakfast bites...nice on a brunch table too!

10-oz. tube refrigerated flaky
 layered biscuits
1/2 c. mayonnaise
1 c. shredded Swiss cheese
1/4 c. onion, chopped

1 t. dried basil
8 slices bacon, crisply cooked
 and crumbled
10-oz. can diced tomatoes and
 green chiles, drained

Separate each biscuit into 3 layers. Press each layer into a lightly greased mini muffin cup; set aside. Combine remaining ingredients in a bowl; mix well and spoon into biscuit cups. Bake at 375 degrees for 10 to 12 minutes. Makes 2 dozen.

If you have leftover eggnog, use it to make French toast the next morning...simply scrumptious!

White Chocolate-Cranberry Scones

Sheryl Eastman
Keego Harbor, MI

These scones are really good! Surprise a friend with a basket of fresh-baked scones, or treat yourself before a busy day of shopping and decorating.

1-1/2 c. biscuit baking mix
2 T. sugar
1/2 c. fresh cranberries, chopped, or sweetened dried cranberries
1/2 to 3/4 c. white chocolate chips

Optional: 1 t. orange zest
1 egg, beaten
3 to 4 T. milk
Optional: powdered sugar

In a large bowl, gently toss together baking mix, sugar and cranberries. Mix in chocolate chips and zest, if using; set aside. In a small bowl, whisk together egg and milk; add to baking mix. Use a fork to mix together gently. With a large cookie scoop, portion out 8 scoops of dough onto a parchment paper-lined baking sheet. Flatten each scone slightly, using moistened hands. Bake 400 degrees for 10 minutes, or until edges are turning golden. Drizzle Orange Glaze over cooled scones; dust with powdered sugar, if desired. Makes 8 scones.

Orange Glaze:

1/2 c. powdered sugar   1 to 2 t. orange juice

Combine powdered sugar with enough orange juice to make a drizzling consistency.

Share your homemade goodies with a friend. Wrap muffins or scones in a tea towel and tuck them into a basket along with a jar of jam. A sweet gift that says "I'm thinking of you!"

Holiday Breakfast & Brunch

Ice Cream Sticky Buns

Marlene Burns
Swisher, IA

Scrumptious and oh-so easy to make! Sprinkle with chopped pecans for even more deliciousness.

1-lb. loaf frozen bread dough, thawed
1 c. vanilla ice cream, melted

1-1/2 c. butter, melted
1-1/2 c. brown sugar, packed
1-1/2 c. sugar

Divide dough into 4 parts; cut each part into 9 pieces and set aside. Combine remaining ingredients in a bowl. Mix well and pour into a greased 13"x9" baking pan. Arrange dough pieces over ice cream mixture. Cover and let rise in a warm place for one hour. Uncover; bake at 375 degrees for 22 minutes. To serve, invert pan onto a plate. Makes 3 dozen.

Breakfast with Santa! Ask a family friend to play Santa for the children at your holiday brunch. They'll love sharing secrets with the jolly old elf over waffles and hot cocoa. At the party's end, have Santa hand out little bags of "Reindeer Food"...cereal mixed with colored jimmies for kids to sprinkle on the lawn on Christmas Eve.

Cozy Christmas
COMFORTS

Easy Scrambled Eggs

Shelley Turner
Boise, ID

We love this easy way to serve the whole family tender scrambled eggs at the same time! Add flavor with a sprinkle of cheese or herbs.

1 doz. eggs	1 t. salt
3/4 c. milk	1/4 t. pepper

In a large bowl, whisk together eggs, milk, salt and pepper. Pour into a lightly greased 13"x9" glass baking pan. Bake, uncovered, at 350 degrees for 7 minutes, or until eggs begin to set. Remove from oven. Use a spatula to gently pull eggs completely across the pan, forming large soft curds. Bake for another 12 to 15 minutes, pulling eggs with spatula a few more times, until thickened and set. Serve immediately. Serves 6.

Brown Sugar-Glazed Bacon

Lynn Williams
Muncie, IN

Irresistible! Sprinkle with cayenne pepper if you like it spicy.

1 lb. thick-sliced bacon, cut in half if desired	1/3 to 1/2 c. brown sugar, packed

Set a wire rack on an aluminum foil-lined baking sheet. Arrange bacon slices on rack in a single layer. Sprinkle evenly with brown sugar; set aside. Position an oven shelf in top third of oven. Bake at 400 degrees for 15 to 18 minutes, until bacon is crisp and glazed. Let cool for 5 minutes before serving. Makes 8 servings.

My idea of Christmas, whether old-fashioned or modern,
is very simple...loving others.
– Bob Hope

Holiday Breakfast & Brunch

Maple-Glazed Breakfast Links

Robin Hill
Rochester, NY

So easy...so good!

2 6-oz. pkgs. precooked
   breakfast sausage links
1 c. pure maple syrup

1/2 c. brown sugar, packed
1 t. cinnamon

Brown sausage links in a skillet according to package directions; drain. Combine remaining ingredients in a bowl; drizzle over sausages. Bring to a boil. Reduce heat to medium-low. Simmer, uncovered, until sausages are glazed. Serves 10.

Spicy Hot Cocoa

Courtney Stultz
Weir, KS

In the cold winter months, we enjoy hot cocoa almost daily. We like trying different versions and this is my favorite. It is sure to warm you up fast!

1/4 c. chocolate bar, chopped,
   or chocolate chips
1 c. whole milk or almond milk

1 t. honey
1/8 t. ground ginger
1/8 t. cayenne pepper

In a small saucepan, melt chocolate over low heat; stir in remaining ingredients. Bring to a low boil, stirring often, until hot. If desired, blend with an immersion blender until frothy. Pour into a mug. Makes one serving.

Just for fun, set out snowman-shaped marshmallows
to float in hot cocoa.

Cozy Christmas
COMFORTS

Fruit Bruschetta

Jo Ann
Gooseberry Patch

This simple recipe is sure to be welcome on holiday brunch tables.

1 c. fresh pineapple, strawberries
   and/or kiwi, diced
1/2 c. sour cream
2 T. honey

1 t. lemon zest
2 t. lemon juice
3 English muffins or bagels,
   split, toasted and buttered

Combine fruit in a bowl; set aside. Combine remaining ingredients in a
separate bowl; mix well. To serve, divide fruit mixture among muffins
or bagels; drizzle with sour cream mixture and serve immediately.
Serves 3 to 6.

Grandma's china and Mom's silver...if not now, when will you
use them? Make the holiday even more special by dressing up
your table with sentimental, handed-down favorites.

Holiday Breakfast & Brunch

Cheesy Potato Breakfast Casserole

Michele Eavey
Lafayette, IN

A wonderful one-dish breakfast. Try switching it up with browned sausage instead of ham, or go meatless by using sliced mushrooms.

1 lb. cooked ham, diced
1/4 c. onion, diced
1/4 c. green pepper, diced
3 c. shredded Cheddar cheese

6 eggs, beaten
2 c. milk
28-oz. pkg frozen diced
  hashbrowns, thawed

In a large bowl, whisk together eggs and milk. Stir in onion, green pepper, cheese and ham; fold in thawed hashbrowns. Pour mixture into a lightly greased 13"x9" baking pan. Cover with aluminum foil. Bake at 350 degrees for 45 minutes. Uncover; bake for another 30 minutes, or until eggs are set. Serves 10 to 12.

Breakfast Egg Spread

Cathy Hiller
Salt Lake City, UT

Spread on toast and go...perfect for the light eaters in my family!

6 eggs, hard-boiled, peeled
  and halved
1/4 c. ranch sour cream dip
2 T. green onion, sliced
1/4 t. salt

1/4 t. pepper
2 T. real bacon bits
baguette slices, toasted
  and buttered

Combine eggs, ranch dip, green onion, salt and pepper in a food processor. Process until finely chopped. Spoon into a serving bowl; top with bacon. Serve with toasted baguette slices. Makes about 1-3/4 cups.

For a great morning time-saver, keep frozen chopped onions and peppers on hand.

Cozy Christmas
COMFORTS

Banana-Sour Cream Coffee Cake
Nancy Johnson
LaVerne, OK

*This tender coffee cake is great with morning coffee. At Christmas,
I like to bake this in mini aluminum foil loaf pans to give as Christmas
gifts. A friend said after she sliced it, she spread butter on each side
and toasted the slices on a hot griddle. Yum!*

1/2 c. shortening
1-1/4 c. sugar, divided
2 eggs, beaten
1 c. ripe bananas, mashed
1 t. vanilla extract
1/2 c. sour cream

2 c. all-purpose flour
1 t. baking powder
1 t. baking soda
1/4 t. salt
1/2 c. chopped pecans
1/2 t. cinnamon

In a large bowl, combine shortening and one cup sugar; stir until light
and fluffy. Beat in eggs, banana and vanilla; stir in sour cream and set
aside. Combine flour, baking powder, baking soda and salt in a separate
bowl. Add to shortening mixture and stir just enough to blend; set aside.
Combine pecans, cinnamon and remaining sugar. Sprinkle half of pecan
mixture into the bottom of a well-greased 10" Bundt® pan; spoon half
of batter into pan. Sprinkle remaining pecan mixture over batter; spoon
remaining batter into pan. Bake at 350 degrees for 40 to 45 minutes,
until cake tests done with a toothpick inserted near the center. Cool cake
in pan on a wire rack for 5 minutes. Loosen edges of cake with a knife,
if necessary. Turn out cake onto a serving plate; serve warm or cooled.
Serves 12 to 15.

A tiered cake stand looks inviting and saves
table space too! Fill alternate levels with
bite-size goodies and Christmas greenery,
tucking in some shiny ornaments for
holiday sparkle.

Holiday Breakfast & Brunch

Pineapple-Nut Coffee Cake

Sandra Mirando
DePew, NY

Delicious and easy to make.

2 c. all-purpose flour
1-1/2 c. sugar
1 t. baking soda
1/2 t. salt

1 egg, beaten
2 c. crushed pineapple, drained
1/2 c. brown sugar, packed
1/2 c. chopped walnuts

In a large bowl, combine flour, sugar, baking soda, salt, egg and pineapple. Mix well; pour batter into a greased and floured 13"x9" baking pan. In a separate bowl, mix brown sugar and nuts; sprinkle over batter. Bake at 325 degrees for 30 minutes. Meanwhile, prepare Topping about 10 minutes before cake is done. Spoon hot topping over hot cake as soon as it is removed from oven. Makes 12 servings.

Topping:

1 c. evaporated milk
1/2 c. butter, sliced

3/4 c. sugar
1/2 t. vanilla extract

Mix together evaporated milk, butter and sugar in a saucepan. Boil over medium-low heat for 2 minutes. Stir in vanilla.

Once again, my dear people,
Merry Christmas is here,
With holly and mistletoe
And its good will and cheer!
– Gertrude Tooley Buckingham

Cozy Christmas
COMFORTS

Nutmeg Streusel Muffins

Althea Rogers
Rancho Cucamonga, CA

This recipe came from a co-worker at my first job...I have been making these muffins for over 25 years now! They are a real family favorite. At the first sign of cooler weather, I make these yummy muffins...they are always a big hit!

2 c. all-purpose flour, divided
1 c. brown sugar, packed
1/2 c. chilled butter, cut into
    chunks
2/3 c. buttermilk

1 egg, beaten
1-1/2 t. baking powder
1/2 t. baking soda
1-1/2 t. nutmeg
1/2 t. salt

Combine 1-1/3 cups flour and brown sugar in a large bowl. Cut in butter with a pastry blender or fork until mixture resembles coarse crumbs. Set aside 1/2 cup for streusel topping. To remaining mixture in large bowl, add remaining flour and other ingredients; stir just until moistened. Spoon batter into 12 greased or paper-lined muffin cups, filling 2/3 full. Sprinkle with reserved streusel topping. Bake at 400 degrees for 18 to 22 minutes, until lightly golden. Let stand 5 minutes; remove from pan. Makes one dozen.

Most muffin batters can be stirred up the night before, and can even be scooped into muffin cups. Simply cover and refrigerate...in the morning, pop them in the oven. Your family will love waking up to the sweet smell of muffins baking!

Maple Crunch Oatmeal

Vickie
Gooseberry Patch

This nutty, crunchy topping makes your morning oatmeal a real treat. We enjoy it on steel-cut oatmeal...yum!

1/4 c. chopped almonds
1/3 c. chopped walnuts
2 T. sunflower kernels
1/2 t. cinnamon
1/4 t. nutmeg
1 T. butter, melted

6 T. pure maple syrup, divided
4 servings favorite oatmeal
1/2 c. sweetened dried
   cranberries
Garnish: milk

Combine nuts, sunflower seeds, spices, butter and 2 tablespoons maple syrup in a bowl; mix well. Spread in a single layer on a parchment paper-lined baking sheet. Bake at 375 degrees for about 12 minutes, stirring every 5 minutes, until mixture is fragrant and toasted, about 12 minutes. Remove from oven; cool. Meanwhile, prepare oatmeal according to package directions; stir in cranberries and remaining maple syrup. To serve, divide oatmeal into 4 bowls; divide glazed nut mixture among bowls and top with milk. Makes 4 servings.

Hide a small wrapped gift in the Christmas tree for each member of the family to find when putting away the ornaments.

Cozy Christmas
COMFORTS

Farmhouse Chicken Pie

Tangela Moore
Spring Hill, FL

My whole family loves this pie! It's a great addition to
a midday brunch...delicious for dinner too.

9-inch pie crust, unbaked
1/2 bunch broccoli, chopped
3/4 c. shredded Swiss cheese
5 slices bacon, crisply cooked
   and crumbled
1-1/2 to 2 c. cooked chicken,
   shredded

2 eggs, beaten
2-1/4 c. milk
1-1/2 T. all-purpose flour
1/8 t. nutmeg
1/8 t salt

Bake pie crust according to package directions. Meanwhile, place
broccoli in a saucepan with a small amount of water; cook over low
heat until tender. To assemble, layer cheese, bacon, broccoli and
chicken in baked pie crust; set aside. In a bowl, combine remaining
ingredients; whisk together well and pour over top. Bake at 350 degrees
for one hour, or until bubbly and crust is golden. Let stand several
minutes; cut into wedges. Makes 5 to 6 servings.

Planning a midday brunch? Along with breakfast foods like baked eggs,
coffee cake and cereal, offer a light, savory main dish for those
who have already enjoyed breakfast.

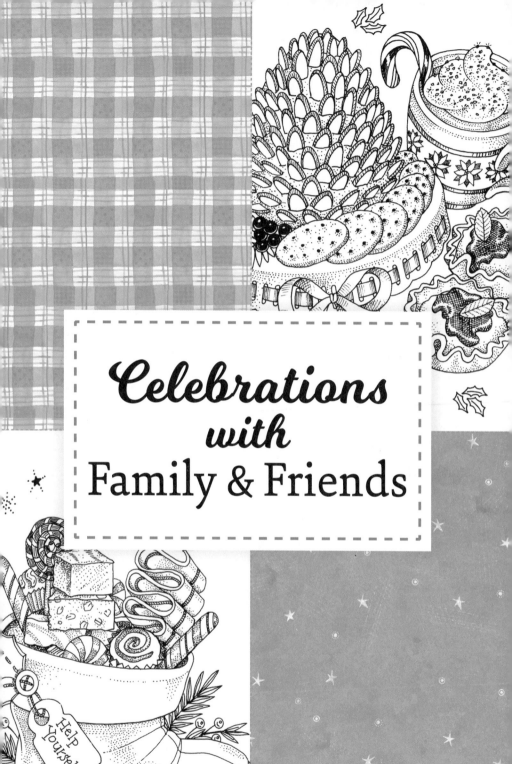

Celebrations
with
Family & Friends

Help Yourself

Cozy Christmas
COMFORTS

Holiday Hot Spiced Cider

Beverley Williams
San Antonio, TX

No Christmas celebration would be complete without a mug of this hot cider! It is my family's favorite way to warm up around the Christmas tree while we sing carols together.

1 gal. apple cider
1/4 c. light brown sugar,
   packed
1 t. allspice

1/8 t. nutmeg
2 t. whole cloves
1 small orange
Optional: cinnamon sticks

Pour cider into a large pot over medium heat. Add brown sugar, allspice and nutmeg; cook and stir until brown sugar is dissolved. Press the points of the cloves into the orange; add to cider. Bring to a low boil; reduce heat to medium-low. Cover and simmer for 20 minutes. Discard orange. Serve cider hot in mugs, garnished with cinnamon sticks, if desired. Serves 16.

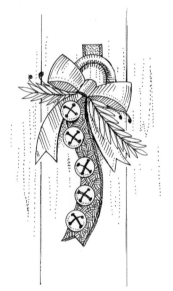

Ring out a holiday greeting to visitors! Hang a string of jingling sleigh bells on the front door.

Celebrations with Family & Friends

Spicy Party Nuts

Gretchen Brown
Hillsboro, OR

I found this recipe in a magazine years ago. These nuts are zesty and make a great gift!

3/4 c. sugar, divided
1/2 t. ground ginger
1 T. cinnamon
1/2 t. nutmeg

1/16 t. cayenne pepper
1/4 c. butter
3 c. salted mixed nuts
1 t. water

Cover a 15"x10" jelly-roll pan with wax paper; set aside. In a large bowl, combine 1/4 cup sugar and spices; set aside. Melt butter in a skillet over medium heat; stir in nuts, water and remaining sugar. Cook and stir over medium heat until sugar dissolves and nuts start to turn golden, about 10 minutes. Add nuts to spice mixture in bowl, tossing to coat; spread on pan. Cool completely; break into small pieces. Store in a tightly covered container. Makes 3 cups.

Roasted Pecans

Sherry Page
Akron, OH

These savory pecans are wonderful for munching.

2 T. butter
2 T. oil

salt to taste
1 lb. pecan halves

Combine butter and oil on a 15"x10" jelly-roll pan. Bake at 250 degrees until butter melts; sprinkle with salt. Spread pecans over pan in a single layer. Stir to coat with butter mixture. Bake at 250 degrees for one hour, stirring every 15 minutes. Sprinkle with additional salt, if desired. Cool; store in an airtight container. Makes about 4 cups.

Spiced nuts are great for snacking...
chop them for a delicious salad
topping too.

Cozy Christmas
COMFORTS

Spicy Beef Spread

Jessica Clark
Oak Grove, MO

My mother has made this recipe at the holidays for as long as I can remember. My sister and I have always scrambled to be the first one to dig in and to be the one to take leftovers home...if there were any, that is! Don't leave out the green onions, they're the best part!

8-oz. pkg. cream cheese, softened
1/4 c. mayonnaise
1 T. horseradish sauce
1-1/2 t. mustard
1/4 t. garlic salt

3-oz. pkg. thin-sliced corned beef, diced
4 green onions, green part only, diced
assorted crackers

In a large bowl, with an electric mixer on medium speed, beat cream cheese and mayonnaise until smooth. Beat in horseradish, mustard and garlic salt. Add corned beef and onions; mix thoroughly. Cover and refrigerate for at least one hour. Serve with crackers. Makes 8 servings.

Invite everyone to a tree-trimming party! Lay out a simple buffet of finger foods and put Christmas carols on the stereo... what could be easier or more enjoyable?

Celebrations with Family & Friends

Herbed Cheese Spread

Joslyn Hornstrom
Elgin, IL

A delicious savory spread I've been making for years. My entire family looks forward to this at the holidays! It's quick & easy when the busy holidays are upon us. Feel free to adjust the seasonings.

8-oz. container whipped cream
   cheese, room temperature
1/2 c. whipped butter, room
   temperature
1-1/2 t. fines herbes seasoning
1 t. dried parsley

1/2 t. garlic powder
1/4 t. Italian seasoning
1/8 t. dried dill weed
1/8 t. salt
1/8 t. white or black pepper

In a large bowl, blend cream cheese and butter. Stir in seasonings until completely blended. Transfer to a bowl with a tight-fitting lid. Cover and refrigerate for several days before serving, to allow the flavors to blend. Keeps well, covered and refrigerated, for up to 2 weeks. Serves 16.

For a hostess gift that's sure to be appreciated, fill a basket with
a crock of a favorite spread and a package or two of crackers.
Tuck in a spreader and tie on a big bow...all set to go!

Cozy Christmas
COMFORTS

Dried Fruit & Cream Cheese Roulade

Joyce LaMure
Sequim, WA

*The original recipe for this unusual spread was given to me
by a neighbor, and I adapted it to my family's taste.
I've had many friends ask for it.*

8-oz. pkg. cream cheese,
  softened
1 T. apricot or apple jelly
1 to 1-1/2 t. water
1/4 c. sweetened dried
  cranberries, chopped
1/4 c. dried apricots, chopped

1/4 c. chopped dates
1/2 c. crumbled feta cheese or
  mild goat cheese
1/3 c. chopped pecans or
  almonds
1 T. fresh chives, chopped
assorted crackers

Place cream cheese between 2 sheets of plastic wrap. With a rolling pin,
roll into a 10-inch by 7-inch rectangle. Remove top sheet of plastic
wrap; set aside. In a small bowl, mix jelly and enough water make it
spreadable. Carefully spread jelly over cheese. Sprinkle with fruits to
within 1/2 inch of edges; sprinkle with crumbled cheese. Starting on
one long edge, carefully roll up cheese mixture into a log, lifting with
the bottom sheet of plastic wrap. Carefully press nuts onto outside of
log, rolling slightly to cover all sides. Wrap tightly in plastic wrap.
Refrigerate at least 2 to 3 hours, until set. To serve, unwrap log and
place on a serving plate; sprinkle with chives. Serve with assorted
crackers. Serves 15 to 18.

Let's dance and sing and make good cheer,
For Christmas comes but once a year.
– Sir George Alexander Macfarren

Celebrations with Family & Friends

Cranberry Roll-Ups

Leona Krivda
Belle Vernon, PA

A very simple and easy appetizer...your guests are sure to love it!

8-oz. container whipped cream
    cheese, softened
8-oz. pkg. crumbled feta cheese
4 green onions, thinly sliced

6-oz. pkg. sweetened dried
    cranberries, chopped
Optional: 2 T. chopped pecans
4 10-inch flour tortillas

In a large bowl, combine all ingredients except tortillas; mix well. Spread mixture evenly on tortillas; roll up. Wrap each in plastic wrap; refrigerate overnight. At serving time, slice each roll into one-inch pieces; arrange on a serving platter. Makes 3 to 4 dozen.

Warm Brie Spread with Topping

Delores Lakes
Mansfield, OH

There's never any left when I serve this...the plate is almost licked clean! Instead of cranberries, you can substitute fig jam or jelly, another flavor of jam or even honey.

8-oz. round Brie cheese
2 T. sweetened dried cranberries
1 t. fresh thyme, chopped

1 T. chopped walnuts, toasted
assorted crackers

Using a serrated knife, remove top rind from cheese; discard rind. Place cheese in an ungreased one-quart casserole dish, cut-side up. Sprinkle with cranberries and thyme; top evenly with walnuts. Bake, uncovered, at 350 degrees for 15 minutes, or until cheese is soft and warm. Serve immediately with crackers. Serves 8.

Keep hot appetizers toasty in a 250-degree oven until serving time.

Cozy Christmas
COMFORTS

Slow-Cooker Chicken-Artichoke Dip

Cheryl Culver
Coyle, OK

Get your veggies in a delicious way with cheese...yes, please!
My mom taught me how to make this several years ago and
we've been enjoying it ever since.

16-oz. pkg. frozen spinach,
  thawed and well drained
2 14-oz. cans artichoke hearts,
  drained, rinsed and coarsely
  chopped
2 c. cooked chicken, cubed
1 c. shredded mozzarella cheese
1 c. shredded Swiss cheese
15-oz. jar Alfredo sauce

8-oz. pkg. cream cheese,
  softened
1/2 c. mayonnaise
4 cloves garlic, minced
1 T. lemon juice
1/2 c. grated Parmesan cheese
1 t. paprika
toasted French bread slices or
  snack chips

In a 4-quart slow cooker, combine all ingredients except Parmesan
cheese, paprika and bread or chips. Mix well. Cover and cook on low
setting for 3 to 4 hours. At serving time, sprinkle with Parmesan cheese
and paprika. Serve with toasted French bread slices or chips. Makes
24 servings.

If your fireplace isn't in use during the holidays, dress it up
to look warm and inviting. Fill an empty grate with cheerful
wrapped packages, candles of every shape and size or
snowy-white birch logs accented by shiny ornaments.

Celebrations with Family & Friends

Out-of-This-World Corn Dip

Sharon Jones
Oklahoma City, OK

Delicious! So easy to mix up and bake, and it makes enough for a crowd.

3 11-oz. cans sweet corn and
   diced peppers, drained
7-oz. can chopped green chiles
6-oz. can chopped jalapeño
   peppers, partially drained
1 c. mayonnaise

1 c. sour cream
1 t. pepper
1/2 t. garlic powder
16-oz. pkg. shredded sharp
   Cheddar cheese
tortilla chips

Combine all ingredients except cheese and chips in a lightly greased 2-quart casserole dish. Mix well; fold in cheese. Bake, uncovered, at 350 degrees for 15 to 20 minutes, until heated through and cheese is melted. Serve warm with tortilla chips. Makes 10 to 12 servings.

For stand-up parties, make it easy on guests by serving foods that can be eaten in just one or 2 bites. Try cherry tomatoes filled with creamy herb dip, mini bruschetta toasts and guacamole spooned into scoop-type tortilla chips.

Cozy Christmas COMFORTS

Crab-Stuffed Mushrooms

Lisa Zamfino
Fairfield, CT

Years ago, I made this recipe the first time I hosted Christmas in my new home. I invited some new friends and their families from the neighborhood, as well as my own family. These mushrooms went so quickly, I didn't have time to take one for myself! Whenever I see this recipe in my recipe book, the memory of that Christmas makes me smile.

36 to 40 cremini mushrooms
2 cloves garlic, minced
1/2 c. dry white wine or
    vegetable broth
8-oz. pkg. cream cheese, cubed
    and softened

6-oz. can crabmeat, drained
    and flaked
1/2 c. green onions, chopped
1/4 c. grated Parmesan cheese
1/2 t. pepper
1/8 t. cayenne pepper

Remove stems from mushroom caps. Finely chop stems, measuring about one cup; set aside. Coat a large non-stick skillet with non-stick vegetable spray; heat over medium-high heat. Add mushroom stems and garlic; sauté for 3 minutes, stirring often. Stir in wine or broth; cook until liquid evaporates. Remove from heat; let cool for 3 to 5 minutes. Add remaining ingredients; stir until smooth. Spread cheese mixture evenly into mushroom caps. Arrange on a lightly greased baking sheet. Bake at 425 degrees for 25 minutes, or until mushrooms are tender and lightly golden. Serve warm. Makes about 3 dozen.

Add pizzazz to an appetizer tray...glue tiny Christmas balls onto long toothpicks for serving.

Celebrations with Family & Friends

Great-Grandma Hattie's Cocktail Meatballs

Monica Britt
Fairdale, WV

This is the recipe my great-grandmother used to make for family get-togethers when I was a kid. Now, 40 years later, I'm still using this recipe when I host family get-togethers!

2 lbs. ground beef
1 egg, beaten
3/4 c. onion, chopped
1/2 t. salt
1/2 t. pepper
12-oz. bottle chili sauce
1 c. grape jelly

In a large bowl, combine beef, egg, onion and seasonings. Mix well; shape mixture into one-inch meatballs and set aside. Combine sauce and jelly in a large saucepan. Cook over medium heat until well mixed. Add meatballs; simmer over low heat for one hour. Makes 20 to 30 servings.

Brown Sugar Sausages

Irene Robinson
Cincinnati, OH

Children and adults love these yummy little sausages.

14-oz. pkg. smoked cocktail
   sausages
1 lb. bacon, cut into thirds
3/4 c. brown sugar, packed

Wrap each sausage in a piece of bacon; fasten with a wooden toothpick. Arrange on an aluminum foil-lined baking sheet; sprinkle with brown sugar. Bake at 325 degrees for 30 to 40 minutes, until bacon is crisp. Makes 10 to 12 servings.

Fill a big glass jar with vintage-style candies...guests of all ages will love scooping out their favorites!

Cozy Christmas
COMFORTS

Sassy Sangria Splash

Kimberly Hancock
Murrieta, CA

Wow...you all have to try this! When we served it at a get-together, everyone loved it. It's perfect for sipping at any festive occasion. I served it in a clear glass pitcher, and the color of the drink and the floating citrus slices are just gorgeous. If you're feeling especially festive, you can substitute rosé wine for the grape juice.

4-1/2 c. sparkling red grape
   juice, chilled
12-oz. can frozen pink lemonade
   concentrate, thawed
1/3 c. lime juice

2 c. club soda, chilled
1 lime, thinly sliced
1 lemon, thinly sliced
ice cubes

In a large pitcher, combine grape juice, lemonade concentrate and lime juice. Stir to combine. If not serving immediately, cover and refrigerate. Just before serving, slowly stir in club soda; add lemon and lime slices. Serve over ice. Makes 10 servings.

Nestle a punch bowl in an evergreen wreath...tuck in fresh red carnations on picks as an accent. So pretty and sweet smelling too!

Sicilian Nachos

Sonya Labbe
West Hollywood, CA

A lot of my friends are Italian, so I wanted to come up with an Italian twist on nachos to serve at parties. This was a hit! For a delicious variation, use ground chicken and chicken broth.

2 T. olive oil
1 lb. ground beef
1/2 c. red onion, finely chopped
1/2 c. carrot, peeled and finely chopped
4 cloves garlic, minced
1 t. cayenne pepper, or to taste
1 bay leaf
1/2 c. dry red wine or vegetable broth

15-1/2 oz. can crushed tomatoes
8-oz. can tomato sauce
1/2 c. vegetable broth
salt and pepper to taste
2 T. fresh basil, chopped
15-oz. pkg. corn or tortilla chips, divided
2 c. shredded Parmesan cheese, divided

Heat olive oil in a large saucepan over medium-high heat. Add beef; cook until browned and a little crisp, 10 to 12 minutes, breaking up beef with a spoon. Push beef to one side of pan; add onion, carrot, garlic, red pepper flakes and bay leaf to the other side of pan. Cook until vegetables are softened, about 5 minutes. Add wine or broth; scrape up browned bits from bottom of pan. Increase heat to high; add tomatoes with juice, tomato sauce, broth, salt and pepper. Cook until mixture begins to thicken, 6 to 7 minutes. Remove from heat; discard bay leaf and stir in basil. Spread half of chips on a rimmed baking sheet; top with half of sauce and half of cheese. Repeat layering. Bake at 350 degrees for just a few minutes, until cheese is melted. Serve hot. Serves 8.

Tuck a string of tiny white lights into a flower arrangement for extra sparkle. Battery-operated sets make it simple.

Cozy Christmas
COMFORTS

Jack's Taco Party Mix

Melissa Mishler
Columbia City, IN

This is such a different party mix...I've never tasted anything like it! I just had to get the recipe and make it myself. It is so delicious, you just can't stop snacking on it!

4 c. bite-size crispy rice
    cereal squares
4 c. doughnut-shaped oat cereal
2 c. chow mein noodles
2 c. salted peanuts

1/2 c. butter, melted
1/3 c. brown sugar, packed
1-1/4 oz. pkg. taco seasoning
    mix

In a large bowl, combine cereals, noodles and peanuts; toss to mix and set aside. In a small bowl, stir together remaining ingredients. Drizzle over cereal mixture; toss to coat well. Spread mixture on a 15"x10" jelly-roll pan sprayed with non-stick vegetable spray. Bake at 300 degrees for 10 to 15 minutes. Stir; bake for an additional 10 to 15 minutes. Cool; store in an airtight container. Makes 12 cups.

Paper baking cups are perfect for serving up party-size scoops of spiced nuts and snack mix.

Celebrations with Family & Friends

Cowboy Caviar

Angela Mayhew
Dumferline, IL

*I love this recipe because it is super-quick & easy,
yet also healthy. Everyone loves it!*

1.05-oz. pkg. Italian salad
   dressing mix
14-1/2 oz. can diced tomatoes
   with green chiles
16-oz. can black-eyed peas,
   drained
15-1/2 oz. can black beans,
   drained and rinsed

15-oz. can white shoepeg
   corn, drained
1 bunch green onions,
   finely chopped
1 red pepper, diced
1 yellow pepper, diced
scoop-type corn chips

In a large bowl, prepare salad dressing mix according to package directions, using either the regular version or the lighter version. Add tomatoes with juice and remaining ingredients except chips. Stir to combine. Cover and refrigerate for at least 4 hours to blend flavors. Serve with corn chips. Makes 10 to 12 servings.

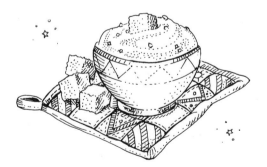

Get together with 3 or 4 friends and have an appetizer swap!
Each makes a big batch of her favorite dip, spread or finger food,
then meet to sample and divide 'em up. You'll all have a super
variety of goodies for holiday parties.

Cheesy Hot Bacon Dip

Sherry Lochner
Wichita, KS

This is our favorite dip at our house! We get requests for it for parties too. It is rich, but oh-so good! This would be easy to lighten up with light mayonnaise, sour cream and cream cheese. If you prefer, warm the bowl of dip in the microwave until hot, then spoon into the bread bowl.

1 lb. bacon
1 c. mayonnaise
1 c. sour cream
8-oz. pkg. cream cheese,
  softened
1 c. shredded sharp Cheddar
  cheese

2 green onions, chopped
1 tomato, chopped
Optional: 1 round loaf Hawaiian
  sweet bread
assorted crackers

In a large skillet over medium heat, cook bacon until crisp. Drain bacon on paper towels; chop into pieces. Meanwhile, in a large bowl, blend together mayonnaise, sour cream, cheeses and green onions. Fold in bacon and tomato; set aside. Cut off top of loaf; hollow out loaf to create a bowl. Spoon dip into loaf; set loaf on a baking sheet. Bake, uncovered, at 350 degrees for 20 minutes. Serve with cubed bread from loaf and assorted crackers. Serves 10 to 12.

For a sparkly centerpiece in a jiffy, arrange shiny vintage balls in a glass trifle bowl. As easy as it gets!

Celebrations with Family & Friends

Merry Crisps Crackers

Janis Parr
Ontario, Canada

These festive little homemade crackers are perfect to serve
alongside a cheese ball or topped with your choice of toppings.
They stay crisp and are very tasty.

1 c. all-purpose flour
1/2 t. baking powder
1/4 t. paprika
1/4 t. seasoned salt

1/3 c. plus 1 T. water, divided
3 T. oil
1 egg white, beaten
Optional: poppy seed to taste

Combine flour, baking powder and seasonings in a bowl. Stir in
1/3 cup water and oil until a smooth dough forms. Cover and chill for
30 minutes. On a floured surface, roll out dough to a 14-inch by
12-inch rectangle. Using small cookie cutters, cut dough into shapes.
Place on greased baking sheets. Whisk together egg white and
remaining water; brush over tops of unbaked cut-outs. Sprinkle with
poppy seed, if desired. Bake at 400 degrees for 6 to 8 minutes, just
until edges begin to turn golden. Cool completely on a wire rack.
Makes 6 dozen.

Sweet-and-Sour Kielbasa

Leona Krivda
Belle Vernon, PA

I have made this so often for lots of different occasions, and everyone
has always loved it. I have given this recipe out many, many times!

3 lbs. Kielbasa sausage, sliced
    into 1/2-inch pieces
20-oz. can pineapple chunks

12-oz. bottle chili sauce
1-3/4 c. brown sugar, packed

Place Kielbasa in a lightly greased 3-quart casserole dish; set aside.
In a bowl, combine pineapple with juice, chili sauce and brown sugar;
mix well and pour over kielbasa. Stir to coat well. Cover and bake at
375 degrees for one hour, stirring occasionally. Serve with party picks.
Serves 12 to 15.

Laughter is brightest where food is best.
– Irish Proverb

Cozy Christmas
COMFORTS

Classic Party Mix

Tina Wright
Atlanta, GA

This is it...the party mix everyone just had to have in the 1960s.
My grandmother shared the recipe with my mom. Now I make it for
all our family's holiday get-togethers. Such tasty memories!

3 c. bite-size crispy wheat or
   corn cereal squares
2 c. bite-size crispy rice cereal
   squares
1-1/2 c. salted peanuts or
   mixed nuts

1-1/2 c. thin pretzel sticks
1/2 c. butter, melted
2 T. Worcestershire sauce
1-1/4 t. seasoned salt
1/4 t. garlic salt

In a large bowl, combine cereals, nuts and pretzels; toss to mix and
set aside. Combine remaining ingredients in a cup; mix well and drizzle
over cereal mixture. Mix well until all pieces are evenly coated. Spread
mixture evenly on 2 ungreased rimmed baking sheets. Bake at
275 degrees for 40 minutes, stirring every 10 minutes, until toasted
evenly. Cool; store in an airtight container. Makes 8 cups.

Fill a big holiday tin with Classic Party Mix for a gift
that just about anyone would love to receive!

Celebrations with
Family & Friends

Cranberry-Dark Chocolate Trail Mix

Nancy Johnson
LaVerne, OK

A friend gave me a delicious trail mix I could not find anywhere later. So one day, looking at the ingredients, I realized I had everything listed on hand. This is the result...one of my favorite snacks! I've made several batches for Christmas gifts and received many compliments.

10-oz. pkg. dark chocolate chips
   or chunks
6-oz. pkg. sweetened dried
   cranberries

5-oz. pkg. sliced almonds
1 c. walnuts, coarsely chopped
1 c. raisins
Optional: 1/2 c. pistachios

Toss together all ingredients in a large bowl. Store in an airtight container. Makes about 7 cups.

You will get a sentimental feeling when you hear
Voices singing, let's be jolly;
Deck the halls with boughs of holly!
– Johnny Marks

Cozy Christmas
COMFORTS

Jan's Simple Cheese Ball

*Jan Abney
Salem, MO*

*Every time our family gets together, they ask me to make
my cheese ball. It's delicious...a real crowd-pleaser!*

8-oz. pkg. cream cheese, room
   temperature
8-oz. pkg. shredded mild or
   sharp Cheddar cheese
1 t. garlic powder, or to taste
1 stalk celery, finely chopped
1/4 green pepper, finely chopped
1/4 onion, finely chopped

1 T. dried parsley
1 T. diced pimentos, drained
Optional: 1/2 c. carrot, peeled
   and very finely chopped,
   or 1/2 c. walnuts, very
   finely chopped
assorted snack crackers

In a large bowl, mix all ingredients except carrot or walnuts and
crackers. Shape into one to 2 balls. Roll in chopped carrot or walnuts,
or leave plain. Wrap in plastic wrap and chill. At serving time, place on
a serving plate; surround with crackers. Serves 8 to 10.

Pop a big bowl of popcorn, snuggle under a quilt and enjoy
a classic Christmas movie with your family.

Celebrations with Family & Friends

Stuffed Potato Skins

Betty Bashaw
Dublin, OH

We've been making these scrumptious potatoes for New Year's Eve for years! They are great for game-day snacking, or add a salad for a fun movie night supper.

6 russet baking potatoes
1 T. oil
1-1/2 c. shredded Cheddar
   cheese
2 green onions, green tops
   only, minced

1/4 lb. bacon, crisply cooked
   and crumbled
Garnish: sour cream

Bake potatoes at 425 degrees for one hour, or until fork-tender. When cool enough to handle, cut in half lengthwise. Scoop out pulp, creating 1/4-inch shells. (Save pulp for another use.) Brush potato skins inside and out with oil; arrange on a baking sheet. Bake 30 minutes longer, turning after 15 minutes. Top evenly with cheese, onions and bacon. Return to oven until cheese has melted, about 5 minutes. Serve with sour cream on the side. Serves 6.

Jubilee Bubbly Punch

Julie Perkins
Anderson, IN

Serve up a sweet and tangy punch that's new to your guests.

2 15-oz. cans jellied cranberry
   sauce
1-1/2 c. orange juice

1/2 c. lemon juice
2 1-ltr. bottles ginger ale,
   chilled

In a large pitcher or punch bowl, whisk cranberry sauce until smooth. Stir in orange juice and lemon juice. Chill until serving time. Just before serving, add ginger ale. Serves 15.

Keep fruit punch from becoming diluted, with an ice ring made of juice! Just freeze cranberry or pineapple juice in an angel food cake pan and pop it out.

Cozy Christmas
COMFORTS

Carlsons' Festive Crab Dip

Tracie Carlson
Richardson, TX

*We have made this for our holiday gatherings for more than 30 years...
and sometimes in between! Sometimes, if I've started with fresh crab,
I like to form the dip into the shape of a crab, and arrange the crab
legs and claws on it. Add a couple of black olive "eyes" and voilà, you
have crab dip, literally! Warning...it won't last long, and everyone will
want the recipe!*

8-oz. pkg. cream cheese,
   softened
1 to 2 t. fresh chives, chopped
1/2 t. garlic powder
3/4 c. dungeness or snow
   crabmeat, cooked and cleaned

1 c. pecans, toasted and finely
   chopped
assorted crackers, cut-up
   vegetables

In a bowl, thoroughly blend cream cheese, chives and garlic powder.
Gently fold in crabmeat. Cover and refrigerate for 2 hours. Form mixture
into a ball or log; roll in pecans. For best flavor, chill for 8 hours to one
day before serving. Serve with assorted crackers and vegetables. Makes
12 servings.

Make a party tray of savory appetizer tarts...guests will never suspect
how easy it is! Bake frozen mini phyllo shells according to package
directions, then spoon in a favorite creamy dip or spread.

70

Celebrations with
Family & Friends

Ruth's Crawfish Dip

Ruth Hebert
Crowley, LA

Louisiana Cajuns like their food hot and spicy...this definitely meets their taste! Serve with crackers, or spoon into mini pastry shells.

2 onions, finely chopped
1/4 c. butter
1 lb. crawfish tails, thawed if
    frozen
10-3/4 oz. can cream of
    mushroom soup

1/2 c. fresh flat-leaf parsley,
    chopped
1 t. Worcestershire sauce
salt and pepper to taste
hot pepper sauce to taste

In a skillet over medium heat, sauté onions in butter until tender. Add remaining ingredients except hot sauce; cook and stir until heated through. Transfer to a chafing dish or slow cooker set on warm; sprinkle with hot sauce. Serves 15.

Kim's Shrimp Spread

Kim Burrell
Manitoba, Canada

I got this recipe from a friend and changed it a bit for our own taste. It's great! I've been making this for Christmas for 20 years.

2 8-oz. pkgs. cream cheese,
    room temperature
2 T. mayonnaise
1 green onion, finely chopped

1/2 lb. cooked shrimp, peeled
    and chopped
buttery round crackers or
    bagel chips

Combine cream cheese, mayonnaise and onion in a bowl; mix well. Add shrimp; mix gently. Cover and refrigerate for 2 hours or overnight. Serve with crackers or bagel chips. Makes 20 servings.

Festive ice cubes! Drop a couple of cranberries and a sprig of mint into each section of an ice cube tray. Fill with distilled water for crystal-clear cubes and freeze.

Cozy Christmas
COMFORTS

Sweet & Tangy Corn & Black Bean Salsa

Leslie Harvie
Simpsonville, SC

My cousin gave me this recipe a couple of years ago, and I have made it for every party and holiday gathering ever since. I usually double the recipe because everyone loves it so much!

1-1/2 c. frozen corn, thawed
    and drained
15-1/2 oz. can black beans,
    drained and rinsed
3 green onions, chopped

1 red pepper, diced
2 T. sugar
1/4 c. cider vinegar
1/4 c. olive oil
tortilla chips

In a large bowl, stir together corn, beans, onions and pepper. Add sugar, vinegar and oil; stir well to combine. Cover and refrigerate at least one hour before serving. Serve with tortilla chips. Makes 6 to 8 servings.

Cut out bite-size pieces of fresh red and yellow pepper with a star-shaped mini cookie cutter...what a clever way to trim a veggie dip platter!

Cool Fiesta Dip

Pat Beach
Fisherville, KY

*Our family loves this quick & easy dip! There's never any left
when I take it to family get-togethers.*

8-oz. pkg. cream cheese,
   softened
16-oz. container sour cream
1-1/2 oz. pkg. taco seasoning
   mix
1/2 head iceberg lettuce, torn
   into small pieces

8-oz. pkg. shredded sharp
   Cheddar cheese
2 to 3 tomatoes, chopped
Optional: 3.8-oz. can sliced
   black olives, drained
tortilla or corn chips

Combine cream cheese, sour cream and taco seasoning in a large bowl.
Beat with an electric mixer on medium speed until well blended. Spread
mixture in a lightly greased 13"x9" glass baking pan. Top with lettuce,
cheese, tomatoes and black olives, if using. Serve immediately, or cover
and chill until serving time. Serve with tortilla or corn chips. Makes
10 to 12 servings.

Looking to lighten up your favorite dips? Try using 1/3 less fat
cream cheese or Neufchatel cheese instead of regular cream cheese.
Just as creamy and good, but much better for you!

Cozy Christmas
COMFORTS

Cream Cheese, Dried Fig & Walnut Spread

Gail Blain
Grand Island, NE

The combination of the figs and walnuts in this appetizer is super yummy! The best part, though, is that it's quick & easy to whip up during the hectic entertaining season.

6 dried figs, quartered and
   stems trimmed
8-oz. pkg. cream cheese, room
   temperature
1/2 t. salt
1/2 c. chopped walnuts, toasted
toasted pita chips, apple or
   pear slices

Finely chop figs in a food processor. Add cream cheese; process until combined. Add salt and walnuts; pulse just to blend. Transfer to a serving bowl; cover and chill until serving time. Serve with toasted pita chips and apple or pear slices. Makes 2 cups.

Pineapple Cheese Spread

Sharon Wilson
Charles Town, WV

This dip is always requested by my family & friends whenever we have parties and family gatherings. It's an unlikely combination of ingredients, but there are never any leftovers because it's so good. Very easy to make when you're busy!

2 8-oz. pkgs. cream cheese,
   room temperature
1/2 c. green pepper, diced
1/2 c. onion, diced
8-oz. can crushed pineapple
buttery crackers, pretzel chips

Combine cream cheese, green pepper and onion in a large bowl; blend well. Add pineapple with juice; mix together well. Cover and refrigerate at least 2 hours, or overnight for the best flavor. Serve with crackers or pretzel chips. Serves 10.

Celebrations with Family & Friends

Roasted Red Pepper Dip

Betsy Flannery
Eagleville, PA

This recipe is as close to zero points as you can get, yet it really tastes great! Perfect when you're trying to get the New Year off to a healthy start.

8-oz. container fat-free
   sour cream
1/4 c. roasted red peppers,
   drained and chopped
2 T. sliced green onions, sliced

2 cloves garlic, minced
1/4 t. dried basil
Italian seasoning to taste
carrot and celery sticks or
   low-fat wheat crackers

In a large bowl, mix together all ingredients except vegetable sticks and crackers. Cover and refrigerate for 4 to 24 hours. Stir again before serving. Serve with carrot and celery sticks or crackers. Makes 12 servings.

White Bean Pesto Dip

Sharon Jones
Oklahoma City, OK

This recipe is absolutely easy to make and so tasty. I love that it has just a few ingredients.

4 cloves garlic, peeled
2 15-1/2 oz. cans cannellini
   beans, drained
1/4 c. basil pesto sauce

2 T. olive oil
juice of 1 lemon
1 t. sea salt
pita chips or crackers

Pulse garlic in a food processor or blender. Add remaining ingredients except chips or crackers. Process until well mixed but still chunky. Serve with pita chips or crackers. Serves 8.

Keep a folder or drawer for clippings from magazines and newspapers...look for easy recipes, fun menus and party ideas you'd like to try. As the holidays approach, you'll be ready!

Cozy Christmas COMFORTS

Christmas Confetti Spread

Sue Coppersmith
Granbury, TX

This delicious, colorful spread can be served as a dip with crackers or sturdy chips or used to make finger sandwiches. It's easy to put together quickly for a last-minute gathering.

3/4 c. cream cheese, softened
1/2 c. mayonnaise
1/2 c. pecans, finely chopped

1 c. sliced or chopped salad
   olives, drained and
2 T. liquid reserved

Combine all ingredients in a covered container; mix well. Cover tightly; refrigerate up to 2 weeks. Serve as a snack dip or sandwich spread. Makes 6 to 8 servings.

This veggie-packed topiary will certainly "spruce" up your buffet table! Cover a 12-inch styrofoam cone with aluminum foil. Attach broccoli flowerets and cherry tomatoes by sticking one end of a toothpick into the veggie and the other end into the cone. Garnish with cheese "ornaments" cut out with mini cookie cutters...clever!

Celebrations with Family & Friends

Spinach-Artichoke Bread

Madonna Alexander
Normal, IL

We have always loved warm spinach-artichoke dip at our family get-togethers. Several years ago, I tried it on some French bread... it was a big hit! I started incorporating Asiago cheese into this recipe. It really gives it a richer flavor.

10-oz. pkg. frozen chopped
    spinach
14-oz. jar artichoke hearts,
    drained and chopped
1 c. mayonnaise
4 to 6 cloves garlic, minced

1/2 c. grated Parmesan cheese
1 c. shredded Asiago cheese,
    divided
1 loaf French bread baguette,
    halved lengthwise

Cook spinach according to package directions; cool and squeeze out as much liquid as possible. In a bowl, combine spinach, artichokes, mayonnaise and garlic. Add Parmesan cheese and 1/2 cup Asiago cheese; mix well and set aside. Place baguette halves on a broiler pan, cut-side up; broil until golden. Spread artichoke mixture evenly over baguettes; sprinkle with remaining Asiago cheese. Return to broiler and broil until cheese is bubbly. Remove from oven. Let stand for several minutes before slicing. Serve immediately. Makes 10 to 20 slices.

Tuck battery-operated tealights and pillars into favorite votives, sconces and centerpieces for a safe, soft glow.

Cozy Christmas
COMFORTS

Sweet & Spicy Chicken Wings

Tracee Cummins
Georgetown, TX

These yummy chicken wings always disappear in a flash!
A favorite for holiday parties or the big game, they're the perfect
blend of sweet and spicy. They are delicious served hot or cold.

1-1/2 T. salt	1/2 c. sugar
1/2 t. pepper	1/2 c. water
1/2 t. garlic powder	1/2 c. lemon juice
1/8 t. cayenne pepper	1/2 c. orange marmalade
3 lbs. chicken wings, separated	1/2 c. butter

Mix together seasonings in a cup; rub into chicken wings. Arrange wings in a single layer on an ungreased shallow 13"x9" baking pan; set aside. Combine remaining ingredients in a small saucepan. Cook and stir over medium heat until butter is melted. Remove from heat; let stand for 10 minutes. Spoon sauce over chicken wings. Bake at 400 degrees for 35 to 40 minutes, until golden and juices run clear when pierced. Serves 8 to 10.

Set up tables in different areas of the house so guests have room
to mingle as they enjoy yummy finger foods and beverages.
Your party is sure to be a festive success!

Quick & Easy Pizza Bread

Paula Marchesi
Auburn, PA

We love football! Over the years, I have accumulated lots of delicious recipes to serve to our game-day friends. I always have this ready in the freezer ready for the next game day, and it seems to go first. Quick, easy and delicious...everyone will enjoy munching on this during the game. Substitute Mexican, Creole or Cajun seasoning if you like.

16-oz. pkg. shredded pizza-
   blend cheese
8-oz. pkg. cream cheese,
   softened
1/4 c. black olives, chopped
1/4 c. mushrooms, chopped

1/4 c. onion, chopped
1/4 c. butter
1-1/2 t. Italian seasoning
1/2 t. garlic powder
3 12-oz. loaves Italian or French
   bread, halved lengthwise

In a food processor, combine all ingredients except bread. Process until mixture is well combined. Spread mixture over cut sides of bread. Arrange bread, cut-side up, on rimmed baking sheets. Bake at 375 degrees for 10 to 12 minutes, until cheese is melted. Cut into slices and serve. To make ahead of time, wrap unbaked bread tightly in plastic wrap and freeze up to one month. To serve, remove from freezer and let stand at room temperature for 30 minutes. Bake as directed. Makes 4 dozen slices.

Toss a red & white patterned quilt over the sofa...
what could be cozier or more welcoming?

Cozy Christmas COMFORTS

Bacon-Cheddar Dip

Beckie Apple
Grannis, AR

*Game day in our house is a big deal! My husband and son count
on me to have all their game-winning snacks ready at kick-off time.
This is a favorite that takes almost no time at all.*

8-oz. container sour cream
1/2 c. mayonnaise
1/8 t. garlic powder
1 lb. bacon, crisply cooked and
   crumbled

8-oz. pkg. shredded Cheddar
   cheese
3 green onions, finely diced
1 to 2 tomatoes, chopped
assorted chips and crackers

In a large bowl, combine sour cream, mayonnaise and garlic powder.
Fold in bacon, cheese, onions and tomatoes. Cover and chill until
serving time. Serve with chips and crackers. Makes 8 servings.

For the easiest-ever tree skirt, simply arrange a length of
brightly colored fabric around the base of the tree.

Warming
Soups &
Breads

Cozy Christmas
COMFORTS

Comfort Chili

Melissa Knight
Elkmont, AL

Growing up in Kentucky, I can remember coming into the house after playing in the snow. My mom would have a huge pot of this chili simmering on the stove. Our family always eats chili with peanut butter sandwiches...try it, please, it is delicious!

3 lbs. ground beef chuck
1 lb. hot ground pork sausage
3 onions, chopped
2 T. garlic, minced
2 T. all-purpose flour
1 T. sugar

1-1/4 oz. pkg. chili seasoning mix
1 t. dried oregano
1 t. salt
2 28-oz. cans whole tomatoes
3 16-oz. cans kidney beans, drained

Combine beef, sausage, onions and garlic in a large soup pot. Cover and cook over medium heat until beef and sausage are no longer pink. Drain; sprinkle with flour, sugar, seasoning mix and seasonings, stirring well. Reduce heat to medium-low. Cover and simmer for one hour, stirring occasionally. Stir in tomatoes with juice and beans; simmer for 20 more minutes. Makes 12 servings.

A simmering kettle of soup fills the house with a wonderful aroma...
so relaxing when you're wrapping gifts or writing Christmas cards.

Warming
Soups & Breads

Friendship Potato Soup

Terri McFayden
Burke, SD

My good friend Sara gave me this recipe 20 years ago. I wasn't a big fan of potato soup until I made this one! Even my children love it. My go-to recipe for soup!

6 potatoes, peeled and cubed
4 carrots, peeled and cubed
3/4 c. onion, chopped
2 to 3 stalks celery, sliced
2 T. chicken soup base, or more
    to taste

salt and pepper to taste
12-oz. can evaporated milk
6 T. butter, sliced
dried parsley to taste

Combine all vegetables in a soup pot; add enough water to cover. Stir in soup base, salt and pepper. Bring to a boil over medium-high heat. Reduce heat to medium and cook until fork-tender. Stir in remaining ingredients. Simmer over low heat for 20 to 30 minutes, until hot. Makes 6 to 8 servings.

Soup suppers are a fuss-free way to get together with friends, neighbors and extended family. Set up a buffet table, decorate simply with holly and greenery and it's all set. Each family brings a favorite soup to share, along with the recipe. What a delicious way to celebrate!

Cozy Christmas
COMFORTS

Chicken & Cheese Soup

Joyceann Dreibelbis
Wooster, OH

*This is such an easy soup to prepare when you're so busy
around the holidays. Very good on a cold, snowy night!*

3 c. potatoes, peeled and cubed
1/2 c. carrots, peeled and diced
1/2 c. celery, diced
1 onion, chopped
4 c. chicken broth
1 c. water
3 cubes chicken bouillon

2 10-3/4 oz. cans cream of
   chicken soup
2 c. deli rotisserie chicken, cubed
2 c. peas
1 c. corn
3/4 lb. pasteurized process
   cheese spread, cubed

In a large saucepan, combine chopped vegetables, chicken broth, water
and bouillon cubes. Bring to a boil over medium-high heat. Reduce heat
to medium; cook until tender. Stir in soup, chicken, peas and corn; cook
for several minutes. Stir in cheese; cook until heated through and cheese
is melted. Serves 8 to 10.

Angie's Potato-Onion Soup

Angela Davis
Guilford, IN

This soup is easy to make and oh-so good...pure comfort!

6 c. chicken broth
3 c. potatoes, peeled and sliced
1 c. green onions, sliced
1 c. white onion, sliced
3 T. fresh parsley, chopped

1-1/2 t. salt
1/8 t. pepper
1 c. half-and-half
Optional: shredded Cheddar
   cheese

In a large saucepan over medium heat, bring chicken broth to a boil.
Add potatoes; return to a boil. Cook for 10 minutes. Reduce heat to
medium; stir in onions. Cook over medium heat for 20 minutes, until
tender. Add parsley, salt and pepper. Process soup in a blender or with
an immersion blender until smooth. Stir in half-and-half. Heat over low
heat until just heated through. Sprinkle individual servings with cheese,
if desired. Serves 4.

Warming Soups & Breads

Easy Cheesy Broccoli Soup

Stephanie D'Esposito
Ravena, NY

My daughters request this soup whenever it is cold and snowy outside. It's even more delicious sprinkled with extra cheese.

12-oz. pkg. frozen chopped broccoli
2 T. butter
1 onion, finely chopped
2 T. all-purpose flour
32-oz. container chicken broth

1 clove garlic, minced
1 c. half-and-half
8-oz. pkg. shredded extra sharp Cheddar cheese
salt and pepper to taste

Cook broccoli according to package directions; drain and set aside. Meanwhile, melt butter in a large soup pot over medium heat. Add onion; sauté until onion is translucent. Sprinkle with flour and stir with a whisk for 2 minutes. Add chicken broth and garlic; cook and stir until thickened. Stir in broccoli, half-and-half and cheese. Stir until cheese is melted. Simmer over low heat for 30 minutes, stirring occasionally. Season with salt and pepper to taste. Makes 4 servings.

Serve toasty baguette chips alongside hot soup. Thinly slice a loaf of French bread. Brush slices with olive oil; place on a baking sheet and sprinkle with grated Parmesan cheese. Bake at 350 degrees until crisp and golden, about 10 minutes. Great with dips and spreads too!

Cozy Christmas
COMFORTS

Fire-Roasted Chili

Mary Thomason-Smith
Bloomington, IN

This slow-cooker chili has become a traditional meal for our family to eat after our church's Christmas choir concert. I put it in the slow cooker in the afternoon, and when we arrive home, the house smells delicious. With sour cream to top, and corn chips on the side, this meal satisfies while we share conversation about the beautiful Christmas music we've enjoyed.

1 T. olive oil
1 onion, chopped
2 cloves garlic, minced
1 lb. ground beef
2 14-1/2 oz. cans diced
    fire-roasted tomatoes
15-1/2 oz. can kidney beans

14-1/2 oz. can tomato purée
1 T. chili powder
2 t. Italian seasoning
1 t. ground cumin
Garnish: sour cream, shredded
    Cheddar cheese

Heat olive oil in a large skillet; sauté onion until slightly softened. Add garlic; cook for one minute. Add beef and cook until browned; drain. Transfer beef mixture to a 4-quart slow cooker. Add remaining ingredients except garnish; do not drain tomatoes and beans. Stir well. Cover and cook on low setting for 4 hours. Serve with sour cream and cheddar cheese as toppings. Serves 6.

Deliver a new stockpot filled with soup ingredients, crackers and a cheese-filled shaker to a neighbor. Be sure to tie on a copy of the recipe! Add a few hearty soup mugs and it's sure to warm up the whole family on a wintry day.

Warming Soups & Breads

Bean & Pasta Soup

Lori Rosenberg
University Heights, OH

Served with warm crusty bread and a chunk of your favorite cheese, this slow-cooker soup is a wonderful winter dinner any day of the week! I like to finish this meal with a hot fruit cobbler.

2 lbs. ground beef, browned
    and drained
2 28-oz. cans diced tomatoes
20-oz. jar spaghetti sauce
3 10-1/2 oz. cans beef broth
4 stalks celery, chopped
3 carrots, peeled and chopped
1 onion, chopped
16-oz. can red kidney beans,
    drained

16-oz. can white kidney beans,
    drained
5 t. dried parsley
3 t. dried oregano
2 t. pepper
Optional: 1 t. hot pepper sauce
8-oz. pkg. favorite short pasta
    shape, uncooked

In a 6-quart slow cooker, combine browned beef, tomatoes with juice and remaining ingredients except pasta. Cover and cook on low setting for 7 to 8 hours, or on high setting for 4 to 5 hours. During the last hour on low, or last 30 minutes on high, stir in pasta. Cover and continue cooking until pasta is tender. Makes 8 servings.

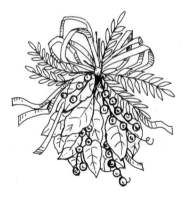

Make a fragrant kissing ball...insert sprigs of fresh rosemary into a foam ball until covered. Pin on a ribbon for hanging and top with a fluffy bow.

Freezer Taco Soup

Carrie Kelderman
Pella, IA

My family loves this zesty taco soup! I love that I can make several batches ahead of time and have them ready in the freezer on a busy day. I also like to keep some batches on hand to give to friends in need of spontaneous acts of kindness.

1 lb. ground beef
1/2 c. onion, chopped
28-oz. can diced tomatoes
15-1/2 oz. can kidney beans
15-oz. can corn

2 T. taco seasoning mix
Garnish: shredded Mexican-
    blend cheese, sour cream,
    diced green onions,
    corn chips

In a large skillet over medium heat, brown beef with onion. Drain; turn off heat. Stir in tomatoes, kidney beans and corn; do not drain vegetables. Add taco seasoning; mix well. Simmer over low heat for 15 to 20 minutes. May serve immediately, or transfer to a freezer container. Seal, label with directions and freeze. To serve, thaw in refrigerator overnight. Heat on the stovetop or in the microwave. Serve soup garnished as desired. Makes 6 servings.

Soups freeze well, so go ahead and make a double batch of your favorites. Freeze half in plastic freezer bags, pressed flat to take less room in the freezer. What a time-saver on a busy day of holiday shopping and decorating!

Warming
Soups & Breads

Mexican Cornbread Muffins

Kimberly Green
Moss Point, MS

I make these muffins for nearly every family get-together...and I usually double the recipe! One weekend, I was making these when my son was home from college, as these are his favorite. He had brought a friend home with him. When his friend walked in, he exclaimed, "Oh my, it smells like Thanksgiving in here!"

1-3/4 c. self-rising yellow
   cornmeal
3 eggs, beaten
3/4 c. oil
1/2 c. milk
1/2 t. salt
1/8 t. pepper
Optional: 1 t. garlic, chopped

1 c. onion, chopped
14-3/4 oz. can creamed corn
12-oz. can whole jalapeño
   peppers, diced and seeds
   removed, if desired
8-oz. pkg. shredded Cheddar
   cheese

In a large bowl, combine cornmeal, eggs, oil, milk, salt, pepper and garlic, if using. Mix well; fold in remaining ingredients. Spoon batter into 24 greased muffin cups, filling 2/3 full. (Paper muffin liners don't work well in this recipe.) Bake at 350 degrees for about one hour, until muffins are golden and start pulling away from sides of cups. Several pans may be baked at the same time. Makes 2 dozen.

Tie ornaments onto the Christmas tree with narrow strips of homespun fabric...sweet and simple!

Cozy Christmas
COMFORTS

Hamburger Comfort Stew

Narita Roady
Pryor, OK

One year, my husband had lost his job and money was tight. We loved stew but couldn't afford stew beef, so I tried hamburger. The recipe sort of evolved. I added some fresh potatoes, onion and celery to go with the frozen mixed vegetables, and Italian seasoning to enhance the stew without overpowering it. It has become a frequent family favorite in chilly weather. Leftovers can be frozen and they warm up great. Delicious with a big pan of warm cornbread!

1 lb. ground beef	1/2 c. water
1/4 c. onion, chopped	14-1/2 oz. can petite diced
2 cloves garlic, minced	tomatoes
1 T. Italian seasoning	8-oz. can tomato sauce
3 stalks celery, chopped	4 cubes beef bouillon
2 to 3 potatoes, peeled and diced	salt and pepper to taste
2 c. frozen mixed vegetables	

In a 6-quart Dutch oven over medium heat, brown beef with onion and garlic. Drain; sprinkle with Italian seasoning. Add fresh and frozen vegetables and water. Cover and simmer until vegetables begin to soften. Add tomatoes with juice, tomato sauce and bouillon cubes. Add enough water to fill pot to within 2 inches from the top. Bring to a boil over medium-high heat; reduce heat to medium-low. Cover and simmer, stirring occasionally, until vegetables are tender, about 45 minutes to one hour. Season with salt and pepper. Makes 8 servings.

Christmas...that magic blanket that wraps itself about us.
– Augusta E. Rundel

Warming
Soups & Breads

Spinach Tortellini Soup

Barbara Bower
Orrville, OH

Winter days bring out the soups, bread and salads at our house. After a cold day of sledding, my children always loved to return home for a warm bowl of soup. Serve in big mugs, with toasted garlic bread on the side.

1 lb. Italian ground pork sausage
3/4 c. onion, chopped
2 to 3 carrots, peeled and diced
1/2 red pepper, diced
3 cloves garlic, minced
1 T. Italian seasoning
6 c. chicken broth
2 8-oz. cans tomato sauce
8-oz. pkg. cheese tortellini,
   uncooked
1-1/2 c. fresh spinach, chopped

Brown sausage in a stockpot over medium heat. Drain; add onion, carrots, red pepper, garlic and Italian seasoning. Cook and stir for 3 to 4 minutes. Add chicken broth, tomato sauce and tortellini; simmer until tortellini is tender. Stir in spinach; simmer 5 more minutes, or until spinach is wilted. Serves 4 to 6.

Parmesan-Garlic Crescents

Cindy Neel
Gooseberry Patch

Delicious with soup or your favorite Italian dish.

8-oz. tube refrigerated
   crescent rolls
3 T. butter, melted
1-1/2 t. garlic powder
1 t. Italian seasoning
2 T. grated Parmesan cheese

Separate crescent dough into 8 triangles. Roll up each crescent from the wide end. Place point-side down on an ungreased baking sheet, 2 inches apart. Curve to form crescent shapes. Combine butter and seasonings; brush over rolls. Sprinkle with cheese. Bake at 375 degrees for 10 to 12 minutes, until golden. Serve warm. Makes 8 rolls.

Cozy Christmas
COMFORTS

Chicken & Butternut Chili

Courtney Stultz
Weir, KS

Some people are very choosy about what goes into a chili recipe. At our house, we just love a good comforting, hearty, tomato-based meal! This non-traditional chili recipe fits the bill. It's loaded with veggies and bold flavors...perfect for cold weather.

2 c. chicken broth
2 c. butternut squash, peeled
    and cubed
1 c. carrots, peeled and diced
2 stalks celery, diced
1 onion, diced
1/2 c. tomato, diced
2 T. tomato paste
1 t. chili powder
1/2 t. ground cumin
1/2 t. cinnamon
1/4 t. paprika
1 t. sea salt
1/2 t. pepper
1 c. cooked chicken, chopped
Garnish: chopped fresh cilantro

In a large stockpot over medium heat, combine chicken broth, squash, carrots, celery, onion and tomato. Cover and cook for about 30 minutes, until vegetables are tender. Stir in tomato paste and seasonings; fold in chicken. Cook for another 5 minutes. Ladle into bowls; sprinkle with cilantro, if desired. Makes 6 servings.

Christmas is for having fun, so gather the whole family in a photo with Santa...a greeting card that will have everyone smiling!

Warming Soups & Breads

Easy White Chicken Green Chili

Jenna Hord
Mount Vernon, OH

My husband isn't a huge fan of beans or tomatoes, so my recipe is skimpy on both. However, the zucchini and quinoa make this a thick, hearty soup, easily made in a slow cooker...great for a busy winter day!

2 c. boiling water
2 cubes chicken bouillon
1 lb. boneless, skinless chicken
    breasts
16-oz. can Great Northern beans
2 jalapeño peppers, diced

1 zucchini, diced
1 c. quinoa, rinsed and uncooked
1 c. salsa verde
3 cloves garlic, pressed
onion powder, salt and pepper
    to taste

Combine boiling water and bouillon cubes in a large cup; let stand until bouillon dissolves. Place chicken in a slow cooker; pour chicken broth over chicken. Add remaining ingredients; stir to mix. Cover and cook on low setting for 8 to 10 hours. At serving time, stir to shred chicken. Serves 4.

When serving soup or chili, offer guests a variety of fun toppings... fill bowls with shredded cheese, oyster crackers, chopped onions, sour cream and crunchy croutons. Then invite everyone to dig in!

Cozy Christmas
COMFORTS

Baked Potato Soup

Sarah Hucks
Orangeburg, SC

This has become our traditional supper on Christmas Eve. After attending the Christmas Eve service at church with my side of our family, we head back to my parents' house for this wonderful soup. After supper, we shoot fireworks for the children to see. Such good memories!

4 baking potatoes	12 slices bacon, crisply cooked
2/3 c. butter	and crumbled
2/3 c. all-purpose flour	1-1/4 c. shredded Cheddar
6 c. milk	cheese
3/4 t. salt	8-oz. container sour cream
1/2 t. pepper	Optional: additional milk

Bake potatoes at 425 degrees for one hour, or until fork-tender. Cut baked potatoes in half; scoop out pulp and set aside. (Reserve potato skins for another use.) Melt butter in a heavy saucepan over medium heat. Add flour; stir until smooth. Cook for one minute, stirring constantly. Gradually add milk. Cook, stirring constantly, until mixture is thick and bubbly. Add potato pulp, salt, pepper, bacon and cheese; cook until heated through. Stir in sour cream and a little extra milk, if the consistency is too thick for your taste. Makes 8 to 10 servings.

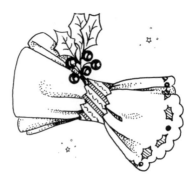

Turn Christmas cards into festive napkin rings. Cut them into strips with decorative-edge scissors, join the ends with craft glue and add a sprig of faux holly...simple!

Warming Soups & Breads

Kale & Sausage Soup

Linda Pitzer
LaPlata, MD

This soup is our favorite! It could be called stew because it's so thick. Serve it with a cake of cornbread and you have all the food groups covered in less than 30 minutes. You can use any kind of sausage you like, and change the kale for spinach or cabbage.

2 T. extra-virgin olive oil
19-oz. pkg. Italian pork sausage
   links, casings removed
Optional: 1/2 c. onion, diced
2 to 3 potatoes, peeled and diced

32-oz. container chicken broth
16-oz. pkg. frozen chopped kale,
   thawed
1 t. dried thyme
salt and pepper to taste

Heat olive oil in a Dutch oven over medium heat; crumble sausage into oil. Add onion, if using; cook until sausage is no longer pink. Add potatoes and cook until golden, but not cooked through. Add chicken broth; bring to a boil. Reduce heat to medium-low. Add kale and thyme; simmer until potatoes are tender. Season with salt and pepper to taste. Makes 4 servings.

Lacy cheese crisps are a tasty garnish for soups. Sprinkle tablespoonfuls of freshly shredded Parmesan cheese onto a baking sheet lined with parchment paper, 4 inches apart. Bake for 5 to 7 minutes at 400 degrees, until melted and golden. Cool and serve.

Cozy Christmas
COMFORTS

Salmon & Corn Chowder

Janis Parr
Ontario, Canada

This is a delicious and comforting soup. You will be asked to share the recipe!

2 T. butter
3 slices bacon
1/2 c. onion, finely chopped
1 stalk celery, finely chopped
3 T. all-purpose flour
2 c. chicken broth
3 potatoes, peeled and diced

1/2 t. dried thyme
salt to taste
1/2 t. pepper
1 bay leaf
7-oz. can salmon, drained
11-oz. can corn, drained
2 c. milk

Combine butter and bacon in a large saucepan over medium heat; cook until bacon is crisp. Break bacon into small pieces; return to saucepan. Add onion and celery; cook for a few minutes, until tender. Slowly add flour; continue cooking over medium heat for about 5 minutes. Stir in chicken broth; bring to a boil. Reduce heat to medium-low; add potatoes and seasonings. Cook until potatoes are tender, about 20 minutes. Break salmon into small chunks, removing any bones; add to soup along with corn and milk. Heat through, but do not boil. Remove bay leaf before serving. Makes 4 to 6 servings.

Make a savory meal even better! Serve up a favorite soup or chowder in hollowed-out round loaves of crusty bread. So cozy shared in front of a crackling fire.

Warming
Soups & Breads

Tasty Seafood Soup

Laura Flood
Markleville, IN

Great on a cold winter night!

1 onion, diced
3 to 4 cloves garlic, minced
3 T. oil
16-oz. pkg. sliced mushrooms
16-oz. pkg. frozen cooked
   shrimp, thawed and tails
   removed

12-oz. pkg. andouille pork
   sausage link, sliced
28-oz. can petite diced tomatoes
16-oz. container chicken broth
1 T. seafood seasoning
salt and pepper to taste

In a large soup pot over medium heat, cook onion and garlic in oil until tender. Add mushrooms and shrimp; cook for 3 minutes. Stir in remaining ingredients, adding chicken broth to desired consistency. Reduce heat to medium-low; simmer for 30 minutes. Makes 6 servings.

Can't-Fail Biscuits

Nancy Wise
Little Rock, AR

Hot from the oven...so good with soup or stew!

2 c. all-purpose flour
4 t. baking powder
2 t. sugar
1/2 t. cream of tartar

1/2 t. salt
1/2 c. chilled butter, diced
3/4 c. milk

In a large bowl, mix all ingredients except butter and milk. Cut in butter until mixture resembles coarse crumbs. Make a well in the center and pour in the milk; stir until dough begins to come together. Turn out onto a lightly floured surface; press dough together. Roll out dough 3/4-inch thick. Cut out biscuits, 2 inches round; place on an ungreased baking sheet. Bake at 450 degrees for 10 minutes, or until golden. Makes about 8 biscuits.

The company makes the feast.
– English proverb

Cozy Christmas COMFORTS

Baked Beef Stew

Sue Hecht
Roselle Park, NJ

After my sister-in-law gave this recipe to my mom, it became a favorite for Sunday dinner. We'd come home from church, and the wonderful aroma was everywhere! That was more than 45 years ago, but whenever I make this stew, that wonderful aroma takes me right back to that beautiful old farmhouse kitchen in Ohio.

2 lbs. lean stew beef cubes
14-1/2 oz. can whole tomatoes,
   cut up and juice reserved
6 carrots, peeled and cut
   into strips
3/4 c. onion, sliced and separated
   into rings

3 potatoes, peeled and quartered
1/2 c. celery, thickly sliced
3 T. quick-cooking tapioca,
   uncooked
1 slice bread, crumbled
1 c. water

Combine beef, tomatoes with juice and remaining ingredients in a greased 3-quart casserole dish or cast-iron Dutch oven. Stir well. Cover and bake at 325 degrees for 3-1/2 hours, stirring occasionally. Serves 6.

Show the children how to make paper snowflakes,
then tape them in the window for a sweet display.

98

Warming
Soups & Breads

Buttery Dinner Rolls

Kathy Symonds
Hanna City, IL

*I received this recipe from my mother-in-law several years ago.
They are requested for all of our family gatherings. Everyone wants
to be the one to take the leftovers home!*

2 envs. active dry yeast
1/2 c. plus 1 t. sugar, divided
1/2 c. very warm water, about
    110 to 115 degrees
3/4 c. butter, softened and
    divided

3/4 c. milk, heated and cooled
2 eggs, beaten
1 t. salt
4 to 5-1/2 c. bread flour

In a cup, mix together yeast, one teaspoon sugar and warm water. Set aside for 5 minutes, or until foamy. In a large bowl, combine remaining sugar, 1/2 cup butter and warm milk. Add eggs, salt and yeast mixture; stir again until mixed. Add flour, one cup at a time; beat with an electric mixer on medium speed after each cup until a soft dough forms. Knead until smooth and elastic. Place in a greased bowl, turning to coat all sides. Cover with plastic wrap. Place in a warm place for one hour, or until double in size. Punch dough down; form into 12 rolls and place on a greased baking sheet. Let rise for 30 minutes. Brush with remaining butter. Bake at 375 degrees for 12 to 15 minutes, until golden. Makes one dozen.

A festive touch for your holiday table...a wreath of rolls!
Arrange unbaked dinner rolls in a ring on a parchment
paper-lined pizza pan. So pretty served on a cake stand.

Cozy Christmas
COMFORTS

Vegetarian Pasta Soup

Karen Augustsson
Hagerstown, MD

This recipe was a last-resort recipe while I was snowed in during the blizzard of 2016 in the Washington, D.C. metro area. I used what I had in the pantry & freezer. This soup can be kept in a slow cooker and will be there for you when you come in from skiing or building your snowman. Great served with a coarse bread.

2 32-oz. containers vegetable
   broth
3 carrots, peeled and sliced
3 stalks celery, sliced
1/2 c. onion, diced
10-oz. pkg. frozen spinach,
   thawed and drained
1 c. peas

6-oz. pkg. whole-wheat
   spaghetti, broken and
   uncooked
15-1/2 oz. can dark red kidney
   beans, black beans or
   black-eyed peas
salt and pepper to taste

In a large soup pot, bring vegetable broth to a low simmer over medium-high heat. Add carrots, celery and onion; cook until carrots are tender-crisp. Stir in spinach and peas; simmer for about 15 to 20 minutes. Add uncooked pasta and beans. Cook for about 10 minutes, until pasta is tender. Season with salt and pepper. Makes 8 to 10 servings.

Winter is a fun-filled, magical time of year...make snow angels,
go sledding, even try ice skating! A wintry bonfire with food,
family & friends will make it a time to remember.
Afterwards, warm up with mugs of hot soup.

Warming Soups & Breads

Healthy Cream of Vegetable Soup

Heather Roberts
Quebec, Canada

I was given this recipe during my first year of university. It is a very low-fat soup, yet so healthy and full of vitamins. Enjoy this smooth tasty soup anytime. It freezes well too!

1 T. butter
1 onion, chopped
1 potato, peeled and chopped
3 cloves garlic, minced
1/2 t. dried thyme
4 c. assorted fresh or frozen
    vegetables, chopped

1-1/2 c. chicken broth
3/4 c. skim evaporated milk
3/4 t. orange zest
1/2 t. salt
1/4 t. pepper

Melt butter in a large soup pot over medium heat; add onion, potato, garlic and thyme. Cook and stir until onion is softened, 5 to 8 minutes. Add vegetables and chicken broth; bring to a boil. Reduce heat to low. Cover and simmer until vegetables are tender, about 15 minutes. Remove from heat; let cool for 10 minutes. Working in batches, transfer soup to a blender or food processor; process until smooth. Return soup to same pot. Add remaining ingredients and heat through for one minute. Serve hot. Serves 4.

Stock your freezer with comforting home-cooked soups and stews, ready to enjoy anytime! They freeze well for up to 3 months in plastic freezer containers. Just thaw overnight in the refrigerator and add a little water when reheating.

Cozy Christmas
COMFORTS

Black Bean-Chicken Stew

Lisanne Miller
Wells, ME

A great hearty stew for a cold winter night! Serve it with lots of delicious toppings and warm bread on the side. You can even thicken it up with a cup or two of cooked orzo pasta.

14-1/2 oz. can diced tomatoes
  with green chiles
28-oz. can tomato purée
2 15-1/2 oz. cans black beans
1/2 c. chicken broth
1 c. frozen corn
1/2 c. frozen chopped onion
1 clove garlic, pressed
1-1/2 lbs. boneless, skinless
  chicken breasts
Optional: cooked orzo pasta
Garnish: shredded Cheddar
  cheese, sour cream,
  corn chips

In a 5-quart slow cooker, combine tomatoes with juice, tomato purée, beans, chicken broth, frozen corn, frozen onion and garlic. Gently push chicken breasts into mixture until covered. Cover and cook on low setting for 4 to 6 hours, until chicken is tender. Shred chicken with 2 forks. If desired, stir in cooked orzo; garnish as desired. Serves 6 to 8.

Make time for your town's special holiday events. Whether it's a Christmas parade with brass bands, Santa arriving by horse-drawn wagon or a tree lighting ceremony downtown, hometown traditions make the best memories!

Warming Soups & Breads

Grandma's Quick Brown Bread   *Carolyn Gochenaur*
Howe, IN

*My Grandma Larimer made this bread often, and we all loved to eat it.
Sometimes just for us, she would cut each slice fairly thin and then in
half. She'd spread one half with butter and make a little sandwich
out of it.*

1 T. shortening, softened	1 c. graham flour
1/3 c. sugar	1 t. baking soda
1/3 c. molasses	1/2 t. salt
1 egg, beaten	1 c. buttermilk
1 c. all-purpose flour	

In a large bowl, blend together shortening, sugar, molasses and egg;
set aside. In a separate bowl, combine flours, baking soda and salt.
Add flour mixture to shortening mixture, alternating with buttermilk;
mix well. Pour batter into a well-greased 9"x5" loaf pan. Bake at
350 degrees for 50 to 55 minutes, until a toothpick inserted in the
center comes out clean. Makes one loaf.

Bring a bit of retro to the holiday kitchen...tie on
a vintage Christmas apron!

Cozy Christmas
COMFORTS

Chicken & Bowtie Pasta Soup

Mary Watkins
Mishawaka, IN

I tasted a soup like this in a restaurant and loved it so much that I made my own version of it within a week. It's very similar, but with my own flair added!

4 c. boiling water
4 t. chicken bouillon granules
1 boneless, skinless chicken
  breast
3 T. olive oil, divided
1/2 c. onion, chopped
2 stalks celery, chopped
2 cloves garlic, chopped

1/4 c. carrots, peeled and
  shredded
1 t. dried thyme
1 t. dried parsley
1 t. salt
1 t. pepper
1 c. bowtie pasta, uncooked
1 c. milk

Combine boiling water and bouillon cubes in a large cup; let stand until bouillon dissolves. Meanwhile, in a large saucepan over medium heat, sauté chicken in 2 tablespoons olive oil until cooked. Remove from pan; set aside. Add remaining oil, onion, celery and garlic; cook until onion is translucent. Add carrots, chicken broth and seasonings. Chop chicken; return to saucepan. Cook until carrots are tender. Add pasta; cook over medium-high heat for about 10 minutes, just until tender. Turn off heat; stir in milk. If preferred, cook pasta in a separate sauce pan in additional chicken broth; stir in pasta at serving time. Makes 4 servings.

Soups & stews stay warm and cozy when ladled into a slow cooker that's turned to the low setting. No matter when family, friends or neighbors arrive for their visit, the soup will be ready to enjoy.

Warming Soups & Breads

Lemony Chicken Soup

Annette Ceravolo
Hoover, AL

This is good with or without spinach and it's quick to make.

1 T. olive oil
1 lb. boneless, skinless chicken
   breasts, cubed
1 onion, diced
4 c. chicken broth, or more
   if needed

1 c. small star pasta, uncooked
Optional: 6-oz. pkg. baby
   spinach
2 T. lemon juice
salt and pepper to taste

Heat oil in large saucepan over medium-high heat; add chicken and onion. Cook, stirring occasionally, about 5 minutes, until chicken is no longer pink. Add chicken broth; bring to a boil. Stir in pasta. Cook for 5 to 7 minutes, until pasta is tender. Stir in spinach, if using, and lemon juice. Season with salt and pepper. Heat through. Serves 4.

Angel Biscuits

Gloria Robertson
Midland, TX

With just three ingredients, these are the easiest biscuits ever!

1 c. self-rising flour
1/2 c. milk

2 t. mayonnaise

Combine all ingredients in a bowl; stir until moistened. Spoon batter into 8 greased muffin cups. Bake at 350 degrees for 15 to 18 minutes, until golden. Serve warm. Makes 8 biscuits.

Treat everyone to honey-pecan butter with warm biscuits. Simply blend together 1/2 cup honey, 1/2 cup butter and 1/3 cup toasted chopped pecans. Delectable!

Cozy Christmas
COMFORTS

Hearty Italian Lentil Soup

Gretchen Grisham
Hillsboro, OR

*Even those who are not a fan of lentils will find this soup
a tasty surprise! My favorite way to serve it is
with a basket of homemade foccaccia bread.*

1 c. dried lentils, rinsed and
   drained
1 lb. ground Italian pork sausage
2 T. olive oil
3/4 c. onion, diced
3/4 c. celery, diced
1 t. garlic, minced
6 c. vegetable or chicken broth
14-1/2 oz. can petite diced
   tomatoes

1 t. Dijon mustard
1 t. dried oregano
1 t. dried basil
2 t. salt
1/2 t. pepper
1/4 t. Worcestershire sauce
2 drops hot pepper sauce
Optional: grated Parmesan
   cheese

Cook lentils according to package directions; drain and set aside.
Meanwhile, brown sausage in a large stockpot over medium heat.
Drain; remove sausage from pot. Add olive oil to pot; heat over
medium-high heat. Add onion, celery and garlic; cook and stir until
softened and golden. Add broth, tomatoes with juice and seasonings.
Stir in cooked, drained lentils and sausage. Heat through for at least
15 minutes. Garnish individual bowls with Parmesan cheese, if desired.
Makes 6 servings.

A snowy winter afternoon is the perfect time to browse seed and
plant catalogs! Relax with a mug of hot tea and start planning
your flower and vegetable gardens for spring.

Green Enchilada Chicken Soup

Sena Horn
Payson, UT

Quick, easy and delicious! It's very good as is, or with toppings to make it extra special. I like to use shredded rotisserie chicken when I can. It makes this easy dish even quicker to whip up on those busy shopping days! It's just as tasty made in a slow cooker...cook on low setting for 6 to 8 hours, and stir in the sour cream 30 minutes before serving.

1/2 c. onion, diced
1 lb. boneless, skinless chicken, diced
1/4 c. oil
14-oz. can chicken broth
28-oz. can green enchilada sauce
2 15-oz. cans Great Northern beans

4-oz. can diced green chiles
1 c. sour cream
salt and pepper to taste
Optional: sour cream, chopped green onions, diced avocados, shredded Cheddar cheese, tortilla chips, lime wedges

In a large soup pot over medium heat, sauté onion with chicken in oil until chicken is cooked thoroughly. Drain; add chicken broth, enchilada sauce, beans and chiles. Simmer over medium heat until warmed through, 10 to 15 minutes. Stir in sour cream; cook over low heat until warmed through. Garnish with toppings as desired. Makes 6 to 8 servings.

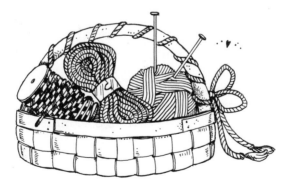

No more ordinary ribbon! Visit a knitting shop for yarns in exciting colors and textures that will make gifts stand out under the tree. Bulky yarns are perfect...thin yarns can be doubled or tripled.

Cozy Christmas
COMFORTS

Black-Eyed Pea Soup

Sara Wyatt
Pratt, KS

I love to make this on New Year's Day to kick off the New Year!
It's a delicious soup to warm the soul on any winter day.

1 lb. dried black-eyed peas
1 lb. ground pork sausage
3 10-1/2 oz. cans beef broth
15-1/2 oz. can diced tomatoes
  with green chiles

1-oz. pkg. onion soup mix
pepper to taste
5 c. water
1 c. long-cooking rice, uncooked

In a large stockpot, cover black-eyed peas with water; soak for 8 hours
or overnight. Drain and rinse peas; return to stockpot. Meanwhile, brown
sausage in a skillet over medium heat; drain and transfer to stockpot.
Stir in beef broth, tomatoes with juice and soup mix; season with pepper.
Add water as necessary to keep the ingredients covered with liquid.
Bring to a boil; reduce heat and simmer for one hour and 30 minutes,
or until beans are tender. Stir in rice during the last 30 minutes of
cooking time. Serves 12.

Ham & Potato-Barley Soup

Becky Kuchenbecker
Ravenna, OH

I love this hearty milk-free soup. It's full of potatoes,
mushrooms, ham and barley...a real stick-to-your
ribs soup for a chilly day!

6 to 8 c. redskin potatoes, cubed
2 4-oz. cans mushroom stems &
  pieces, drained
1/2 c. long-cooking barley,
  uncooked

1 lb. cooked ham, cubed
seasoned salt to taste
2 to 3 T. butter, sliced
Optional: chopped fresh parsley

Combine potatoes, mushrooms, barley and ham in a soup pot; add
enough water to cover. Bring to a boil over high heat; reduce heat to
medium-low. Cook for 1-1/2 to 2 hours, stirring often, until barley is
tender. Add seasoned salt to taste. Just before serving, stir in butter;
sprinkle with parsley, if desired. Serves 6.

Warming Soups & Breads

Stuffed Green Pepper Soup

Katie Bonomo
Ogden, IL

Stuffed peppers made easy! Every time I make this soup for someone, they're begging for the recipe. It comes out perfectly every time! Tastes even better the next day, and freezes well also.

2-1/2 lbs. ground beef
1 onion, chopped
4 cloves garlic, minced
1 T. Worcestershire sauce
2 T. Italian seasoning
2 t. pepper
1 T. chili powder
2 green peppers, chopped

2 red peppers, chopped
28-oz. can tomato sauce
64-oz. bottle tomato juice
32-oz. container beef broth
3 c. instant rice, or 1 lb. acini
    di pepe pasta, uncooked
Garnish: shredded Cheddar
    cheese

In a large stockpot over medium heat, brown beef with onion until no longer pink. Drain; add garlic, Worcestershire sauce and seasonings. Cook for about 5 more minutes. Stir in remaining ingredients except rice or pasta. Bring to a boil; reduce heat to low and simmer for at least 2 hours, stirring every 30 minutes or so. About 30 minutes before serving time, cook rice or pasta according to package directions; drain and add to soup. Cook for about 20 more minutes, stirring often. At serving time, top with cheese. Serves 16.

For a thoughtful gift that's sure to be appreciated, purchase a new calendar. Fill in birthdays, anniversaries and other important family events...a nice gift for those new to the family!

Cozy Christmas
COMFORTS

Chickpea & Sausage Soup

Rosemarie Iliano
Boulder City, NV

I love to create new soups! This Italian-themed soup
is a new favorite of mine.

1 lb. dried chickpeas, rinsed
  and drained
1 to 2 T. olive oil
1 lb. Italian pork sausage links,
  casings removed
3 carrots, peeled and diced
2 stalks celery, diced
1 onion, cut into 1/2-inch cubes
28-oz. can plum tomatoes,
  chopped

4 c. chicken broth
4 c. beef broth
1/4 t. fennel seed
1 head savoy cabbage, quartered
  and sliced
1/2 c. fresh Italian parsley, finely
  chopped
2 to 3 cloves garlic, chopped
Garnish: grated Parmesan cheese

In a large stockpot, cover chickpeas with water. Soak overnight; drain.
Heat olive oil in a large stockpot over medium heat. Add crumbled
sausage; cook until browned. Add carrots, celery, onion, tomatoes with
juice, broth, fennel seed and drained chickpeas. Reduce heat to low and
cook for 1-1/2 hours, or until chickpeas are tender, stirring occasionally.
Add cabbage, parsley and garlic; simmer for 30 minutes. Serve topped
with Parmesan cheese. Makes 8 to 12 servings.

A basket filled with warm & cozy blankets sitting alongside
a stack of favorite holiday stories will invite little ones
to snuggle in for bedtime stories.

Warming
Soups & Breads

Red Lentil Soup

Joanne Novellino
Bayville, NJ

This soup freezes well. Make a double batch and keep some
in the freezer for lunch on a cold winter's day!

1-1/2 c. dried red lentils, rinsed
    and drained
4 c. chicken broth, or more
    as desired
1-1/2 c. onions, minced
3 cloves garlic, minced

1 to 2 carrots, peeled and
    minced
2 T. olive oil
2 bay leaves
pepper to taste
1/4 c. red wine vinegar

In a soup pot over medium-high heat, combine all ingredients except vinegar in a soup pot. Bring to a boil; reduce heat to low. Simmer for 60 to 70 minutes, until lentils are very tender. If desired, thin soup to desired consistency with additional broth; heat through. Discard bay leaves; stir in vinegar and serve. Makes 6 servings.

Pick up some paintable wooden cut-outs in holiday shapes at a neighborhood craft store. They're fun and easy for kids to decorate as package tie-ons that can later be used as tree ornaments.

Cozy Christmas
COMFORTS

Slow-Cooker Chicken Noodle Soup
Ann Davis
Brookville, IN

*Good chicken noodle soup is a must in cold weather. Give this
very easy yet delicious recipe a try...you'll love it!*

3 14-oz. cans chicken broth
10-3/4 oz. can cream of
   chicken soup
2 c. frozen corn, thawed
1/2 c. onion, finely chopped
1/2 c. celery, finely chopped
1/2 c. carrots, peeled and finely
   chopped

1 t. garlic, minced
1/4 t. salt
1 t. pepper
5 boneless, skinless chicken
   breasts
2 c. egg noodles, uncooked

In a 6-quart slow cooker, combine all ingredients except chicken and
noodles; stir well. Gently push chicken into mixture. Cover and cook
on low setting for 7 to 8 hours, until chicken is very tender. Remove
chicken to a plate; cool and shred. Return chicken to slow cooker;
stir in noodles. Cook until noodles are tender, 10 to 15 minutes.
Makes 8 servings.

Gifts of time and love are surely the basic ingredients
of a truly merry Christmas.
– Peg Bracken

Scrumptious
Salads & Sides

Cozy Christmas
COMFORTS

Grandma Miller's Waldorf Salad
Tammy Carnaghi
Westville, IL

This is one of our family's favorites! We had this salad at every Thanksgiving and Christmas. Although my grandma has passed away, I continue the tradition every year and still make it in the very same bowl Grandma used! She always made a separate dish for a cousin who was allergic to nuts.

6 Red Delicious apples, peeled, cored and chopped
3 ripe bananas, chopped
juice of 1/2 lemon
1 c. seedless red grapes, halved

2-1/2 c. mini marshmallows
1 c. chopped walnuts
1-1/2 c. mayonnaise-style salad dressing

Combine apples and bananas in a large serving bowl. Drizzle lemon juice over fruit; toss to coat well. Add grapes, marshmallows and walnuts; toss to mix. Gently mix in salad dressing. Cover and refrigerate for one hour before serving. Serves 8.

March Mason jar luminarias along your front walk. Simply fill canning jars half full with rock salt and nestle tea lights in the salt. The flames will make the rock salt sparkle like ice crystals!

Scrumptious Salads & Sides

Turkey Supper Cranberry Salad

Cindy Akre
Plano, IL

This recipe has been served for many years at our church's annual turkey supper. It is exceedingly popular, and we are often asked for the recipe, which we happily provide. Many of us make it in our homes for Thanksgiving or Christmas.

12-oz. pkg. fresh cranberries
2 c. sugar
3 c. water
6-oz. pkg. cherry gelatin mix

2 c. celery, chopped
2 c. apples, peeled, cored
   and diced
1 c. chopped pecans or walnuts

In a large saucepan over medium-high heat, combine cranberries, sugar and water. Bring to a boil; cook and stir for 5 minutes, or until berries are soft. Add dry gelatin mix and stir well. Remove from heat; allow to cool completely. Stir in celery, apples and nuts; transfer to a serving bowl. Cover and chill until set. Makes 16 servings.

Spinach Pomegranate Salad

Jill Burton
Gooseberry Patch

This unusual salad can be tossed together in just minutes.
Use spring mix instead of spinach, if you like.

10-oz. pkg. baby spinach
1/4 red onion, very thinly sliced
1/2 c. chopped pecans, toasted
1/2 c. crumbled feta cheese

seeds of 1 pomegranate
1/4 c. balsamic vinaigrette salad
   dressing

Place spinach in a salad bowl. Add onion, nuts and cheese; toss to mix. Sprinkle with pomegranate seeds; drizzle with vinaigrette and serve. Serves 4.

For a tasty garnish on salads, use a vegetable peeler
to make cheese curls in a jiffy.

Cozy Christmas
COMFORTS

Susan's Pasta Slaw

Susan Ottinger
Mooresville, IN

I found a variation of this recipe in a cookbook years ago and changed it a bit to make it mine. It's a great make-ahead recipe. Any time I take it to a pitch-in dinner, I am asked for the recipe. It has been served at Thanksgiving, Christmas, Easter, you name it. It goes well with ribs and chicken. A good friend eats it by the bowlful! Be sure to use your best mayonnaise.

12-oz. pkg. tri-color spiral pasta,
  uncooked
16-oz. pkg. shredded
  coleslaw mix
1/2 c. onion, chopped
1/2 t. dried dill weed,
  or to taste

Cook pasta according to package directions; drain and rinse with cold water. In a large bowl, toss together pasta, coleslaw mix, onion and dill weed. Add Dressing and toss to coat. Cover and chill overnight for best flavor. Stir again before serving. Serves 10 to 15.

Dressing:

1/2 c. white vinegar
1 c. sugar
2 c. mayonnaise
2 T. mustard
1/2 t. dried dill weed,
  or to taste

In a bowl, mix vinegar and sugar until sugar is dissolved. Whisk in remaining ingredients until blended, smooth and creamy.

Brush pine cones in craft glue, then roll in cinnamon. Heap in a basket for a rustic accent that smells so good!

Scrumptious Salads & Sides

Shoepeg Corn Salad

Renee Whited
Monterey, TN

This is one of my favorite recipes to take to potlucks and family reunions. It's so tasty that it's hard to believe how simple it is to make! Every time I take this dish, someone requests the recipe.

2 15-oz. cans white shoepeg
    corn, drained
1 cucumber, diced
1/2 c. red onion, or 3 to 4 green
    onions, diced

1 to 2 tomatoes, diced
1/4 c. mayonnaise or
    mayonnaise-style salad
    dressing
salt and pepper to taste

In a large serving bowl, combine corn, cucumber, onion and tomatoes. Stir in mayonnaise or salad dressing. Season with salt and pepper to taste. Cover and chill. Makes 8 servings.

For hearty salads in a snap, keep unopened cans of diced tomatoes, black olives, garbanzo beans and marinated artichokes in the fridge. They'll be chilled and ready to toss with fresh greens and salad dressing at a moment's notice.

Cozy Christmas
COMFORTS

4-Bean Salad

Beverley Williams
San Antonio, TX

My parents used to make this salad often. It is great for any occasion, especially around the holidays. Easy to make ahead, then just pull from the fridge and serve.

15-1/2 oz. can kidney beans, drained and rinsed
15-oz. can garbanzo beans, drained
14-1/2 oz. can cut green beans, drained
14-1/2 oz. can cut yellow wax beans, drained

1/2 green pepper, very finely diced
1/2 c. onion, very finely diced
1/2 c. oil
1/2 c. cider vinegar
3/4 c. sugar
1 t. salt
1/2 t. pepper

Combine all beans, green pepper and onion in a large bowl; mix gently and set aside. In a separate bowl, combine remaining ingredients well. Stir until sugar dissolves; pour over bean mixture. Toss to coat well. Cover and refrigerate overnight, stirring occasionally. Serves 8.

Christmas waves a magic wand over this world, and behold, everything is softer and more beautiful.
– Norman Vincent Peale

Scrumptious Salads & Sides

Cheddar-Broccoli Salad

Hollie Moots
Marysville, OH

At our family dinners, this salad is just called "Hollie's broccoli stuff" and it never lasts long! It's easy to put together and goes well with everything, from Christmas dinner to a summer cookout.

6 c. broccoli flowerets
1-1/2 c. shredded Cheddar
   cheese
1/4 c. red onion, chopped

1-1/2 c. mayonnaise
3/4 c. sugar
3 T. red wine vinegar
3-oz. pkg. bacon crumbles

In a large bowl, combine broccoli, cheese and onion; set aside. In a separate bowl, combine mayonnaise, sugar and vinegar. Stir well; spoon over broccoli mixture and toss to coat. Cover and refrigerate for at least 4 hours or overnight. Just before serving, stir in bacon. Makes 8 servings.

Creamy Pea Salad

Sherre Yurenko
Cypress, CA

I make this simple salad for holidays, potlucks and special events. Everyone loves it and asks me to make it.

2 16-oz. pkgs. frozen peas,
   thawed
1 c. shredded Cheddar or
   Cheddar-mozzarella blend
   cheese

1/2 c. onion, chopped
1 c. mayonnaise
6 slices bacon, crisply cooked
   and crumbled

In a large bowl, combine peas, cheese, onion and mayonnaise. Mix well. Cover and refrigerate until chilled. Just before serving, add bacon and mix well. Makes 14 to 16 servings.

Don't toss out that dab of leftover cranberry sauce! Purée it with balsamic vinaigrette to create a tangy salad dressing.

Cozy Christmas
COMFORTS

Marie's Ribbon Salad

Jennie Gist
Gooseberry Patch

My mom used to make this for Christmas dinner. With its pretty layers of holiday colors, it was always a favorite.

3-oz. pkg. lime gelatin mix
3 c. boiling water, divided
1/3 c. unsweetened pineapple
   juice
1 c. crushed pineapple, drained
1 t. unflavored gelatin
2 T. cold water
8-oz. pkg. cream cheese,
   softened

1/3 c. milk
2 3-oz. pkgs. strawberry or
   raspberry gelatin mix
14-oz. can whole-berry
   cranberry sauce
Garnish: mayonnaise-style
   salad dressing

Green layer: in a small bowl, dissolve lime gelatin mix in one cup boiling water. Stir in pineapple juice and pineapple. Pour into an 11"x7" glass baking pan; refrigerate until set. White layer: in a small saucepan, sprinkle unflavored gelatin over cold water; let stand for one minute. Cook and stir over low heat until completely dissolved; transfer to a large bowl. Beat in cream cheese and milk until smooth. Spread cream cheese mixture over chilled, set lime layer; refrigerate until set. Red layer: in a small bowl, dissolve strawberry gelatin mix in remaining 2 cups boiling water; stir in cranberry sauce. Cool for 10 minutes. Carefully spoon over chilled, set cream cheese layer. Refrigerate until set. To serve, cut into squares; garnish with a dollop of salad dressing. Serves 10 to 12.

Christmas day is a day of joy and charity.
May God make you very rich in both.
– Phillips Brooks

Scrumptious Salads & Sides

Judy's Millionaire Fruit Salad

Judith Smith
Bellevue, WA

This delicious recipe has always been a family tradition. It is a light fruit salad that can be served as part of a holiday meal, or as dessert for those too stuffed for pie. I got the recipe from my 92-year-old mother, who had received the recipe from her mother over 60 years earlier.

2 eggs, beaten
5 T. lemon juice
5 T. sugar
2 T. butter
30 marshmallows, cut up

1 c. whipping cream
3 ripe bananas, sliced
20-oz. can crushed pineapple, drained
16-oz. can fruit cocktail, drained

In the top of a double boiler, combine eggs, lemon juice, sugar, butter and marshmallows. Cook and stir over medium heat until marshmallows melt; let cool. In a bowl, with an electric mixer on high speed, beat cream until soft peaks form. Fold whipped cream into cooled egg mixture. Fold in bananas, pineapple and fruit cocktail. Cover and chill several hours before serving. Serves 10 to 12.

Jalapeño Cranberry Relish

Gail Galipp
Mabank, TX

This relish is wonderful with roast turkey or baked ham! I have made this recipe every Christmas for years for my husband, who likes spicy dishes.

1 to 2 jalapeño peppers, deveined and seeded, if desired
12-oz. pkg. fresh cranberries
1 whole orange, quartered

11-oz. can crushed pineapple, well drained
1 c. sugar

Remove seeds from jalapeños, if a milder taste is preferred. In a food grinder, grind jalapeños, cranberries and orange. Stir in pineapple and sugar; transfer to a serving bowl. Cover and refrigerate overnight before serving. Serves 8 to 10.

Cozy Christmas
COMFORTS

Nana's Potato Salad

Rachel Evans
Beavercreek, OH

My grandmother passed this recipe on to my dad, and he has passed it down to me. I enjoy making my grandmother's recipes, because it keeps her fresh in my memories. She was the most wonderful woman, and I hope you enjoy her recipe as much as our family does.

5 to 6 potatoes, peeled and cubed
salt and pepper to taste
6 eggs, hard-boiled, peeled
    and diced
1 to 2 green onions, sliced into
    1/4-inch pieces

3-oz. jar green salad olives,
    drained and halved
1/2 c. mayonnaise
1 t. mustard

In a large saucepan over high heat, cover potatoes with water. Bring to a boil; cook for 20 to 25 minutes, until fork-tender. Drain; transfer potatoes to a large bowl and allow to cool completely. Season lightly with salt and pepper. Add eggs, onions and olives; mix gently and set aside. In a small bowl, mix mayonnaise and mustard. Add to potato mixture and stir to coat evenly. Cover and refrigerate; serve chilled. Serves 6 to 8.

Save a step by boiling eggs and potatoes at the same time!
Let the potatoes cook in a large pot of boiling water for about
10 minutes, then add the eggs and cook for another 15 minutes.
Remove from heat; drain.

Scrumptious Salads & Sides

Warm Skillet Cabbage Slaw

Terri La Bounty
British Columbia, Canada

Even people who don't usually care for cooked cabbage love this easy-to-make slaw. It's excellent alongside your favorite pork dish.

2 slices bacon
2 T. onion, chopped
1 T. vinegar
1 T. water
1-1/2 t. sugar
1/4 t. salt
1/4 t. pepper

2 c. green and/or red cabbage, shredded
1 apple, cored and chopped
2 T. sweetened dried cranberries or raisins
1/4 c. sour cream or plain yogurt

In a skillet over medium heat, cook bacon until crisp. Remove bacon to a paper towel, reserving drippings in skillet. Sauté onion in drippings for 2 minutes; stir in vinegar, water, sugar, salt and pepper. Bring just to boiling. Add cabbage, apple and cranberries or raisins; cover and cook for 5 minutes. Remove from heat; stir in sour cream or yogurt. Sprinkle with crumbled bacon and serve warm. Makes 4 servings.

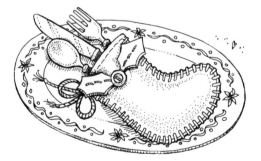

Slip each guest's flatware into a small red felt stocking and lay on dinner plates for a festive table.

Donna's Rigatoni Salad

Donna Guthrie
North Benton, OH

I have been making this salad for over 35 years. It's a favorite of my husband and children...great for Christmas or any time of year. My fondest memory of this salad is of my husband and kids each trying to get the last little bit. Be prepared to pass out copies of the recipe!

16-oz. pkg. bite-size rigatoni
    pasta, uncooked
1 to 2 t. oil
1 onion, diced
1 green pepper, diced

4-oz. jar diced pimentos, drained
4-oz. can sliced black olives,
    drained
1 c. cherry tomatoes

Prepare Dressing; set aside. Cook pasta according to package directions; drain and rinse with cold water. Transfer pasta to a large plastic salad bowl with a tight-fitting lid; toss with oil. Add remaining ingredients except tomatoes. Drizzle with dressing and toss to mix well. Cover and refrigerate for 24 hours, turning bowl every 2 to 3 hours to marinate salad. Add tomatoes just before serving. Serves 8 to 10.

Dressing:

1 c. sugar
1 c. vinegar
1/3 c. oil
2 T. mustard
1 t. garlic powder

1 t. salt
1 t. pepper
Optional: 1 t. powdered flavor
    enhancer

Whisk together all ingredients.

A large clear glass bowl is a must for entertaining! Serve up a layered salad, a fruity punch or a sweet dessert trifle... even fill it with shiny glass ornaments to serve as a sparkly centerpiece.

Scrumptious Salads & Sides

Cheesy Corn Salad

Nancy Davis
Granada Hills, CA

A family favorite...yum! A hearty salad that's perfect for potlucks and get-togethers. I often make a double batch.

4 15-oz. cans corn, drained
8-oz. pkg. shredded Cheddar
   cheese
1-1/2 c. mayonnaise
1/2 c. green pepper, chopped

1/2 c. red pepper, chopped
1/2 c. red onion, chopped
10-oz. pkg. regular or chili
   cheese corn chips, crushed

In a large bowl, combine all ingredients except corn chips; mix well. Cover and chill. Add corn chips just before serving. Serves 8 to 10.

Crunchy Pea & Peanut Salad

Marcia Shaffer
Conneaut Lake, PA

We enjoy this salad when we're watching the game on television.

2 10-oz. pkgs. frozen peas
14-oz. can Spanish peanuts

3/4 c. sour cream
4 t. mayonnaise

Combine all ingredients in a bowl; mix well. Cover and chill until ready to serve. Makes 8 to 10 servings.

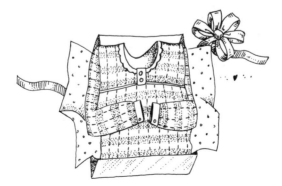

As much fun as when you were a kid...buy new jammies
for everyone spending Christmas Eve at your home!

Cozy Christmas
COMFORTS

Sugar-Free Cranberry Salad

Linda Bare
Mount Carmel, IL

This recipe has been made at Christmas time in our family as long as I can remember...and that is at least 50 years!

2 whole oranges
1 T. orange zest
12-oz. pkg. fresh cranberries
1 red apple, cored and sliced
11-oz. can crushed pineapple
12 envs. powdered sweetener, or to taste

0.6-oz. pkg. sugar-free raspberry gelatin mix
2 c. boiling water
Optional: 2/3 c. chopped pecans

Grate one tablespoon orange zest; peel both oranges. Cut each into 8 slices; remove seeds. Place oranges, cranberries and apple into a food processor. Process until evenly chopped; transfer to a bowl. Add zest, pineapple with juice and sweetener; set aside. In a separate bowl, dissolve gelatin mix in boiling water. Add to fruit mixture; stir well. Fold in nuts, if using. Cover and refrigerate until set. Serves 10.

No-Sugar-Added Applesauce

Marsha Baker
Pioneer, OH

Since my husband and I have to watch our sugar intake, I love that this is naturally sweetened. If preferred, add sweetener after it's cooked. This freezes nicely, but usually doesn't last that long!

12 Cortland, McIntosh or Gala apples, peeled, cored and quartered
1 to 2 4-inch cinnamon sticks

1/3 c. apple juice
1/4 c. agave nectar or honey, to taste

Place apples in a 4-quart slow cooker. Add cinnamon stick; drizzle with agave nectar or honey. Cover and cook on high setting for 2 to 3 hours, or on low setting for 4 to 5 hours, to desired consistency. Discard cinnamon sticks. Stir with a wooden spoon or potato masher for chunky applesauce. For a smoother sauce, process in a food processor or with an immersion blender. Serves 5 to 6.

Scrumptious Salads & Sides

Cranberry-Pear Relish

Marcia Marcoux
Charlton, MA

This is a tasty addition to a holiday buffet table. The spices add a zing to this relish.

1-1/2 c. sugar
1 c. water
1/4 c. lemon juice
4 to 5 ripe pears, peeled, cored
 and chopped

12-oz. pkg. fresh cranberries
1-1/2 t. lemon zest
1/4 t. cinnamon
1/4 t. allspice

In a saucepan over medium heat, combine water, lemon juice and sugar. Bring to a boil; simmer for 5 minutes, stirring until sugar dissolves. Add pears; return to a boil and simmer another 5 minutes. Add cranberries; boil for 7 minutes, or until berries pop. Remove from heat. Stir in lemon zest and spices; allow to cool. Spoon into a container; add lid. May keep refrigerated up to one week. Makes 3 cups.

Holiday Pear Salad

Zoe Bennett
Columbia, SC

This fresh, festive salad is easy to toss together.

4 c. mixed salad greens
2 Anjou or Bosc pears, cored and
 cut into bite-size pieces
1 red onion, thinly sliced

1/2 c. crumbled blue cheese
1/2 c. balsamic vinaigrette
 salad dressing

Toss together all ingredients in a salad bowl. Toss to mix well; serve immediately. Makes 6 to 8 servings.

Cozy Christmas
COMFORTS

Make-Ahead Mashed Potatoes

Laura Weber
San Jose, CA

Whenever I served a holiday dinner for a large gathering, I always had to make mashed potatoes at the last minute to keep them warm. With this recipe, the potatoes can be fixed ahead of time, kept warm in the oven and they taste great! This is the only way I make them now. I have doubled and even quadrupled this recipe, and it has always turned out beautifully.

8 to 10 potatoes, peeled
  and quartered
4 to 5 t. salt
8-oz. pkg. cream cheese,
  softened
1 c. sour cream

1/8 t. baking soda
salt and pepper to taste
Optional: 2 T. fresh chives,
  chopped
1/4 c. butter, diced

Place potatoes in a large stockpot; cover with water and add salt generously. Bring to a boil over high heat; boil for 10 to 15 minutes, or until potatoes are very tender. Drain well; transfer potatoes to a large bowl. Beat with an electric mixer on medium speed. Add cream cheese, sour cream and baking soda. Continue beating until potatoes are fluffy and smooth. Season with salt and pepper; mix in chives, if using. Transfer potatoes to a buttered 13"x9" baking pan; dot with butter. Cover with aluminum foil and refrigerate. At this point, potatoes may be frozen if desired, then thawed before baking. Bake, covered with foil, at 325 degrees for 15 minutes. Uncover and continue baking for about 20 minutes, until crusty on top. Serves 10 to 12.

Candy cane-style napkin rings that are so simple, the kids can make them! Just twist together red and white pipe cleaners and slip napkins inside.

Scrumptious Salads & Sides

Mom's Baked Corn

Charlotte Smith
Alexandria, PA

My mother, who is no longer with us, made this dish for all the holidays. She found it in a 1950s Grange cookbook and seasoned it to her liking. It's my favorite, and it's even good reheated. Yummy!

15-1/4 oz. can corn, drained
14-3/4 oz. can creamed corn
1/2 c. all-purpose flour
1/2 c. butter, softened

1 c. sugar
2 eggs, beaten
1 t. salt
1/2 t. pepper

In a large bowl, combine all ingredients; mix thoroughly. Transfer mixture to a greased 3-quart casserole dish. Cover and bake at 350 degrees for 50 to 55 minutes. Uncover and bake another 10 minutes, or until golden. Serves 6.

Shirred Potatoes

Danielle Vargason
Menifee, CA

My aunt gave me this recipe on one of her many visits...she always brought new ideas and recipes. We had such fun in the kitchen! The long baking time turns this dish into a blend of creamy goodness.

4 to 5 T. butter, divided
1-1/2 T. all-purpose flour
3 c. milk
3 c. potatoes, peeled and grated

salt and pepper to taste
minced onion to taste
Optional: 1/2 c. shredded
    Cheddar cheese

Blend 3 tablespoons butter, flour and milk in a large saucepan over medium heat. Cook, stirring constantly, until thickened into a sauce. Immediately fold in potatoes. Stir in remaining butter; season with salt, pepper and onion. Transfer to a buttered shallow 13"x9" baking pan. Bake, uncovered, at 325 degrees for about 2 hours, until tender and golden. If desired, top with cheese in the last 10 minutes. Makes 4 to 6 servings.

It is Christmas in the heart
that puts Christmas in the air.
– W.T. Ellis

Cozy Christmas
COMFORTS

Daddy's Broccoli Casserole

Suzanne Varnes
Toccoa, FL

This is my dad's broccoli casserole recipe...requested by me every Thanksgiving and Christmas! It's cheesy and delicious. Some cooked, cubed chicken, turkey or ham may be added, if you like.

3 to 4 bunches broccoli, cut into bite-size flowerets
3 T. water
3/4 c. onion, chopped
3 T. olive oil
1/2 c. sliced almonds
8-oz. can sliced mushrooms, drained
3 10-3/4 oz. cans cream of mushroom soup
16-oz. pkg. pasteurized process cheese, cubed
4 t. garlic, minced
1 T. garlic pepper

Place broccoli in a microwave-safe bowl; cover with plastic wrap. Microwave on high for 5 minutes; drain. Transfer broccoli to a greased 13"x9" baking pan; set aside. In a skillet over medium-high heat, sauté onion in olive oil until golden. Remove onion from pan, reserving oil in pan. Sauté almonds in reserved oil until lightly golden. Remove from pan; sauté mushrooms. Add soup and cheese to skillet; stir until well combined and cheese has melted. Return onion and almonds to pan; stir well. Season with garlic and garlic pepper. Pour cheese mixture over broccoli. Cover and bake at 325 degrees for 25 minutes, or until hot and bubbly. Serves 8 to 10.

Trim a mini Christmas tree with tiny ornaments...it's just the right size for a holiday buffet table. Sweet!

Scrumptious Salads & Sides

Yummy Ginger Carrots

Jill Ball
Highland, UT

It wouldn't be dinner at Grandma's house without these tasty carrots!

1 lb. carrots, peeled and sliced
1/4 c. butter
2-1/2 T. honey

1 T. lemon juice
1/8 t. ground ginger

Fill a large skillet with water; bring to a boil over medium-high heat. Add carrots; cook for about 5 minutes, until tender but still firm. Drain; set aside carrots. In same skillet over low heat, melt butter with honey; stir in lemon juice and ginger. Stir in carrots and simmer until heated through. Serve warm. Makes 6 servings.

Lemon-Buttered Green Beans

Jill Valentine
Jackson, TN

An easy way to jazz up simple green beans. You may substitute steamed, fresh green beans for frozen. I like to garnish this with curls of lemon zest.

16-oz. pkg. frozen cut green
    beans
2 T. butter, melted
2 T. lemon juice

1 T. Italian salad dressing
1/8 t. salt
1/4 t. seasoned pepper

Cook green beans according to package direction; drain. Transfer to a serving dish; set aside. In a small bowl, combine remaining ingredients. Mix well and drizzle over green beans. Serves 6 to 8.

Make a quick and yummy cheese sauce for steamed veggies. Combine one cup evaporated milk and 1/2 cup shredded cheese. Cook and stir over low heat until smooth.

Nana's Cornbread Dressing

Glenda Tolbert
Moore, SC

This is my great-grandmother's dressing, and it's delicious. While it bakes, the aroma fills the kitchen...yum! If you prefer, you can use the yellow cornbread mix that comes in the little box.

6 slices whole-wheat bread,
    crumbled
1-1/4 c. onion, finely chopped
1 c. celery, finely chopped
1-1/2 t. ground sage

1 t. salt
pepper to taste
3 eggs, beaten
4 c. chicken broth
Optional: 2 T. butter, melted

Bake Buttermilk Cornbread the day before. Crumble cornbread and place in a large bowl; add crumbled wheat bread and toss to mix. Add onion, celery and seasonings; beat in eggs. Gradually stir in chicken broth and mash well; consistency should be thin. Spread in a greased 13"x9" baking pan. Drizzle with butter, if using. Bake, uncovered, at 350 degrees for one hour. Makes 16 servings.

Buttermilk Cornbread:

2 c. self-rising buttermilk
    cornmeal
1-3/4 c. buttermilk or milk

1/4 c. oil
1 egg, beaten
Optional: 1 to 2 T. sugar

Combine all ingredients in a bowl; mix well. Pour batter into a 9" pie plate. Bake at 425 degrees for 25 to 30 minutes, until golden.

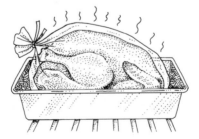

Keep some oven roasting bags on hand for baking holiday ham, chicken or turkey. The bags will speed up the cooking time, plus there's no roaster to clean up...just toss the bag!

Scrumptious Salads & Sides

Sweet Potato Medallions

Anita Mullins
Eldridge, MO

My husband loves sweet potato casserole for holiday dinners,
so I came up with this easier version using his favorite ingredients
from the casserole...brown sugar and pecans.

4 sweet potatoes
1/4 c. butter
3/4 to 1 c. dark brown sugar,
    packed

1/2 c. chopped pecans

Cover potatoes with water in a large saucepan. Bring to a boil over heat; cook until tender but not soft. Drain and let cool; pull off peels. Slice into 1/2 to 1-inch medallions; set aside. Melt butter in a large skillet over medium heat. Add sweet potato medallions; sprinkle with brown sugar and divide pecans evenly among medallions. Simmer until brown sugar dissolves and sweet potatoes are heated through and fork-tender. Serves 4.

Keep a jar of pumpkin pie spice handy if you love its spicy taste.
A blend of cinnamon, ginger, nutmeg and cloves, it's delicious in
side dishes, quick breads and muffins...not just pie!

Cozy Christmas
COMFORTS

Grandma Amelia's Zucchini Casserole

Lori-Marie Ackerman
Freeland, MI

This was my Italian grandmother's favorite way to use zucchini and also became mine as well. It's a very quick and healthy meatless side dish. It is also very good ladled over spaghetti.

3 to 4 small zucchini, cut into
    1-inch chunks
1 to 2 T. olive oil
5 roma tomatoes, halved and
    quartered, or 15-oz. can
    diced tomatoes
2 stalks celery with leaves,
    finely chopped
1/2 c. onion, chopped

1 carrot, peeled and finely
    chopped
1 clove garlic, minced
Optional: 4-oz. can sliced
    mushrooms, drained
1 T. sugar
1 T. dried basil
salt and pepper to taste
Garnish: grated Parmesan cheese

In a lightly greased 2-quart casserole dish, combine all ingredients except garnish. Mix gently. Bake, uncovered, at 350 degrees for 30 to 40 minutes, stirring occasionally, until vegetables are tender. Sprinkle with Parmesan cheese at serving time. Makes 4 to 6 servings.

For a new spin on a traditional Advent calendar, tuck wrapped candies, tiny toys and notes into a stocking garland. A great way to count down the days until Santa's visit!

Grandma Flossie's Wild Rice

Wendy Jo Minotte
Duluth, MN

This mouthwatering dish has a place at every holiday table. Flossie always adds mushrooms to hers, but when I make it, I leave them out. It's up to you!

1 lb. wild rice, uncooked
1 lb. bacon, cut into
    1-inch pieces
3 T. butter
3/4 c. onion, diced
4 stalks celery, diced

1 c. water
2 t. chicken soup base or
    instant bouillon
Optional: garlic powder and
    soy sauce to taste

Soak wild rice overnight in cold water, until puffy. The next day, drain and rinse rice. Add rice to a saucepan; add enough water to cover again. Boil over medium-high heat until rice pops, about 40 to 45 minutes. Drain. Meanwhile, cook bacon in a skillet over medium heat until crisp and golden; drain and set aside bacon. Melt butter in same skillet; sauté onion and celery until crisp-tender. Add one cup water and soup base or bouillon to skillet; stir until well mixed. Stir in rice and bacon. If desired, season with a few shakes of garlic powder and soy sauce. Stir well. Simmer for about 10 minutes. Serves 8.

Pass along Grandma's soup tureen to a new bride...fill it
with favorite seasonings and tie on a cherished soup recipe.
Sure to be appreciated!

Cozy Christmas
COMFORTS

Apple Stuffing

Donna Wilson
Maryville, TN

*I love stuffing with apples! It makes a really tasty
cool-weather side dish to serve anytime with
roast chicken or turkey.*

1 onion, diced
1/2 c. celery, chopped
1 apple, cored and finely diced
6-oz. pkg. chicken-flavored
    stuffing mix

1-1/2 c. applesauce
1 c. chicken broth
2 t. dried thyme
1 t. poultry seasoning
salt and pepper to taste

Spray non-stick skillet with non-stick vegetable spray. Add onion and
celery; cook until onion is translucent. Stir in apple; cook until apple
is tender. Transfer onion mixture to a large bowl; stir in remaining
ingredients. Place in a greased casserole dish. Cover and bake at
350 degrees for 20 minutes, or until heated through. Serves 8.

The more the merrier! Why not invite a neighbor or a
college student who might be spending the holiday
alone to share the Christmas feast with you?

Scrumptious
Salads & Sides

Mom's Harvard Beets

Bobbi Crosson
Toledo, OH

*I grew up loving beets because of this recipe. Quick, inexpensive
and yummy. My mom has been gone for several years now,
yet I still like to make her recipe.*

1 c. sugar
4 t. cornstarch
1/2 c. vinegar

1 T. butter
15-oz. can sliced beets, drained

Combine sugar, cornstarch, vinegar and butter in a saucepan. Cook
over medium heat until thick and sugar dissolves, stirring often. Stir in
beets; heat through. Serve warm, or cover and chill before serving.
Makes 4 servings.

Favorite Festive Cranberry Sauce

Jenny Wright
Carneys Point, NJ

*This recipe is something that I've come up with over the years.
It's perfect to serve with holiday dinners or roast chicken.*

2 12-oz. pkgs. fresh cranberries
2-1/4 c. sugar
1 c. water

zest of 2 large oranges
juice of 1 large orange

In a large saucepan over medium-high heat, combine all ingredients.
Bring to a boil. Reduce heat to medium; cook until berries are soft and
mixture starts to thicken. Let cool slightly; pour into a gelatin mold or
into canning jars. Cover and chill. Makes about 2 quarts.

If you love fresh cranberries, stock up when they're available and
pop unopened bags in the freezer. They'll stay fresh and flavorful
for months to come.

Cozy Christmas
COMFORTS

Creamy Baked Acorn Squash

Shirley Howie
Foxboro, MA

*The flavors of dill and curry give this creamy squash
a delicious flavor. Serving it in the squash halves makes
for an elegant presentation!*

2 acorn squash, halved and
   seeds removed
2 T. butter
6 slices bacon, chopped
1/2 c. onion, chopped
1 stalk celery, chopped

2 T. all-purpose flour
1 T. chicken bouillon granules
1 t. dried dill weed
1 t. curry powder
12-oz. can evaporated milk

Place squash halves cut-side up in a microwave-safe dish. Cover and
microwave on high for 8 minutes, or just until tender. Let stand for
5 minutes. Meanwhile, melt butter in a skillet over medium heat; add
bacon, onion and celery. Cook, stirring often, for about 2 minutes, until
bacon is crisp. Sprinkle with flour, bouillon and seasonings. Cook,
stirring constantly, for 2 minutes longer. Stir in milk and bring to a boil.
Remove from heat. Scrape pulp from squash halves; add to milk mixture
in skillet and mix well. Divide mixture among the squash halves;
arrange in a greased 2-quart casserole dish. Cover and bake at
350 degrees for 15 to 20 minutes, until heated through. Serves 4.

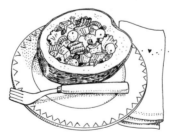

Christmas is not in tinsel and lights...
it's lighting a fire inside the heart.
– Wilfred A. Peterson

Maple Mashed Sweet Potatoes

Chastidy Anderson
Sandusky, OH

This delicious yet simple recipe originated over 50 years ago with my Nana. She made it every year for Thanksgiving and Christmas. The caramelized onion on top makes it special. Now that she has passed on, my mother and I make it, with loving thoughts of her in our hearts.

5 sweet potatoes, peeled
    and cubed
4 T. extra-virgin olive oil
1 t. salt
1 t. pepper

1/2 c. pure maple syrup
1/4 c. butter, divided
1 T. brown sugar, packed
1 sweet onion, sliced

In a large bowl, toss sweet potatoes with olive oil, salt and pepper. Transfer potatoes to a lightly greased sheet pan; drizzle with maple syrup. Bake at 325 degrees for 30 minutes, or until potatoes are very soft. Meanwhile, melt 2 tablespoons butter in a skillet over medium heat; add onion. Cook for 10 minutes, or until dark golden and caramelized. Remove onion from heat and set aside. Transfer hot potatoes to a serving bowl; mash well. Stir in brown sugar and remaining butter. Heap the caramelized onion on top. Makes 6 servings.

Placecards and guest favors all in one! Tape a placecard to the wire loop at the top of a tree ornament and set one at each place setting.

Cozy Christmas
COMFORTS

Cheesy Ranch & Bacon Hashbrown Casserole

Lori Simmons
Princeville, IL

Everybody's favorite potato dish! It's great for brunch as well as dinnertime. Perfect for potlucks. If you'd like to dress it up, top with extra cheese and bacon...bake for another ten minutes.

32-oz. pkg. frozen hashbrown
    potatoes, thawed and drained
10-3/4 oz. can cream of chicken
    soup
8-oz. container sour cream
3/4 c. real bacon bits

1/2 c. onion, chopped
1-oz. pkg. ranch salad dressing
    mix
8-oz. pkg. shredded sharp
    Cheddar cheese

Combine all ingredients in a large bowl; mix well. Transfer mixture to a greased 13"x9" baking pan. Bake, uncovered, at 350 degrees for 35 minutes, or until hot and bubbly. Serves 10.

Christmas
Dinner Menu

Holiday Pork Loin

Grandma's String
Beans

Carrot Casserole

Egg Nog Pie

Planning a big holiday menu packed with homemade goodness? Be sure to include items that are easily made ahead. Many side-dish casseroles can be prepared and frozen as much as one to 2 months in advance, then thawed overnight and warmed as needed.

Gramma's Corn Casserole

LaDeana Cooper
Batavia, OH

This is one of those "mysterious" recipes handed down through the years. We usually make it for holiday dinners, but I have made it on a whim just because it's soooo good and I miss it! If you like corn, you will love this recipe...so will all those picky eaters!

2 14-3/4 oz. cans creamed corn
15-1/4 oz. can corn, drained
1 c. onion, chopped
1 c. celery, chopped

2 eggs, lightly beaten
1 sleeve saltine crackers,
    crushed
salt and pepper to taste

Combine all corn, onion and celery in a large bowl. Add eggs and cracker crumbs; mix thoroughly. Season with salt and pepper. Spoon into a lightly greased 2-quart casserole dish. Bake, uncovered, at 350 degrees for 30 minutes, or until center is set. Allow to cool slightly before serving. Makes 8 servings.

Baked Spinach with Bacon

Diana Chaney
Olathe, KS

A delicious way to serve fresh spinach.

6 slices bacon, cut into
    1-inch pieces
1/2 c. onion, chopped
2 T. red wine vinegar
1/2 t. cinnamon

1 t. salt
1/2 t. pepper
3 lbs. fresh spinach, sliced
    crosswise

In a skillet over medium heat, sauté bacon and onion until bacon is crisp. Remove from heat. Partially drain; stir in vinegar and seasonings. Add spinach and toss to mix. Transfer to a greased 13"x9" baking pan. Cover and bake at 350 degrees for 30 minutes, or until spinach is tender. Serves 6.

Carrying in a casserole? Be sure to tie on a tag with the recipe name! Clever tags can be made from holiday cards cut with pinking shears.

Cozy Christmas
COMFORTS

Calico Stew

Leah-Anne Schnapp
Grove City, OH

I found this recipe more than 40 years ago and gave it a try in an effort to get my children to eat lots of vegetables in one sitting. Success! Serve with baked chicken or pork chops.

1-1/3 c. butter
4 c. potatoes, peeled and cubed
2 32-oz. cans corn, drained
2 c. carrots, peeled and sliced
2 c. onions, chopped

1 T. salt
2 t. sugar
2 t. dill weed
1/2 t. pepper
Optional: 1 to 2 tomatoes, diced

Melt butter in a large saucepan over medium heat. Add remaining ingredients and stir well. Reduce heat to medium-low. Cover and cook for about 20 minutes, stirring often, until vegetables are tender and well blended. If desired, stir in tomatoes when done. Makes 8 servings.

Make some quick & easy fire starters for a frosty winter day. Bundle newspaper into 6-inch squares and secure with natural twine. Tuck under firewood and light with a match...so simple.

Mexican Hominy Hot Dish

Janice Curtis
Yucaipa, CA

*Good as a side dish with just about anything! You'll love
the made-from-scratch cheese sauce.*

25-oz. can Mexican hominy,
   drained
1/2 c. frozen corn
1/4 c. onion, finely minced

1/4 c. roasted mild green chiles,
   chopped
1/4 t. red pepper flakes

Make Cheese Sauce first. Add hominy, corn, onion, chiles and red
pepper flakes to cheese sauce; mix well. Spoon into a lightly greased
13"x9" baking pan. Bake, uncovered, at 350 degrees for about 40 to
45 minutes, until golden and sauce has cooked down slightly. Makes
6 servings.

Cheese Sauce:

3 T. butter
3 T. all-purpose flour
1-3/4 c. milk

8-oz. pkg. shredded Cheddar
   cheese

Stir together butter and flour in a large saucepan over medium heat.
Add milk; cook and stir until sauce thickens. Stir in cheese until melted.

Perhaps the best Yuletide decoration
is being wreathed in smiles.
– Unknown

Cozy Christmas
COMFORTS

Green Bean Bundles

Joyce Roebuck
Jacksonville, TX

This recipe is so easy and oh-so good! Perfect for special occasions.
My family always asks for this when we have family get-togethers.

2 15-oz. cans whole green
  beans, well drained
8 slices bacon, cut in half
1/4 c. margarine, melted
1/4 c. brown sugar, packed

1/2 t. dried mustard
1/8 t. garlic powder
2 T. red wine vinegar
salt and pepper to taste

For each bundle, bunch several beans together and wrap with a 1/2 slice of bacon. Arrange bundles in a lightly greased 13"x9" baking pan. In a small bowl, combine remaining ingredients except salt and pepper. Mix well; spoon over bean bundles. Season with salt and pepper. Cover and bake at 350 degrees for about one hour, uncovering for the last 15 to 20 minutes, until hot and bacon is crisp. Serves 5 to 7.

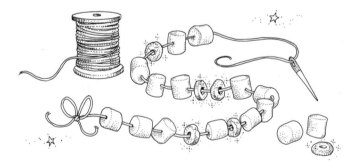

Using mini marshmallows and ring-shaped cereal, sturdy thread and a blunt needle, children will have fun making garlands to wind around the Christmas tree. Much easier for little hands than stringing popcorn!

Home
for the
Holidays

Cozy Christmas
COMFORTS

Easy Turkey Tacos

Jess Brunink
Whitehall, MI

My family loves tacos...we eat these once a week! They're so easy, quick and good. Perfect for a weeknight meal, especially during the busy holiday season.

2 lbs. ground turkey
2 T. canola oil
16-oz. can pinto beans
1/3 c. hot pepper sauce
1/3 c. water
4 t. ground cumin, or to taste

2 t. garlic powder
2 t. onion powder
8 to 10 taco-size corn tortillas
    or taco shells
Garnish: sour cream, salsa,
    chopped onions

In a large skillet over medium heat, cook turkey in oil until browned; drain. Stir in remaining ingredients except tortillas or taco shells and garnish. Cover and simmer over medium-low heat for 15 minutes, stirring occasionally. To serve, spoon turkey mixture into tortillas or taco shells; garnish as desired. Makes 8 to 10 servings.

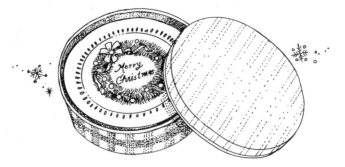

Go ahead and unpack the Christmas tableware early in December...even the simplest meal is festive when served on holly-trimmed plates!

Nacho Chip Casserole

Lynda Hart
Bluffdale, UT

This is a very tasty, quick weeknight dinner dish...kids love it!

1 lb. ground beef
8-oz. pkg. shredded Mexican-blend cheese, divided
10-3/4 oz. can cream of chicken soup
14-1/2 oz. can diced tomatoes with green chiles
1 c. milk

1 c. sour cream
1-1/4 oz. pkg. taco seasoning mix
9-oz. pkg. nacho-flavored tortilla chips, crushed
Garnish: chopped lettuce, diced tomatoes, sliced black olives

Brown beef in a skillet over medium heat; drain. Stir in one cup cheese, soup, tomatoes with juice, milk, sour cream and taco seasoning. Spread a layer of crushed tortilla chips in a greased 2-quart casserole dish; spread half of beef mixture over chips. Repeat layering; top with remaining cheese. Cover and bake at 350 degrees for 30 minutes, or until bubbly and cheese is melted. Garnish servings as desired. Serves 4.

Santa Fe Chicken & Rice Casserole

Donna Snyder
Cumming, GA

One of my family's favorite dinners! This is very easy to fix and can even be prepared a day ahead.

4 boneless, skinless chicken breasts
1/2 c. onion, sliced
1/4 c. butter

14-1/2 oz. can diced tomatoes with green chiles
4 c. cooked rice
1 c. shredded Cheddar cheese

In a saucepan, cover chicken with water. Simmer over medium heat until tender. Cut chicken into bite-size pieces; reserve 1/2 cup of broth from pan. In a small skillet, sauté onion in butter until tender. Combine chicken, reserved broth, onion mixture, tomatoes with juice and cooked rice; spread in a lightly greased 2-quart casserole dish. Top with cheese. Bake, uncovered, at 400 degrees for 30 minutes, until hot and bubbly. Makes 6 servings.

Cozy Christmas
COMFORTS

Sour Cream Noodle Casserole

Emily Hartzell
Portland, IN

Tasty and economical...what more could you want?

8-oz. pkg. wide egg noodles,
   uncooked
1 lb. ground beef
15-oz. can tomato sauce
1 t. dried parsley
1/2 t. salt
1/2 t. pepper

3/4 c. sour cream
1 c. cottage cheese
1 t. onion powder
1/2 t. garlic powder
1 c. shredded Cheddar cheese,
   divided

Cook noodles according to package directions; drain. Meanwhile, brown beef in a skillet over medium heat; drain. Stir in tomato sauce, parsley, salt and pepper. Reduce heat to low; simmer until heated through. In a large bowl, combine sour cream, cottage cheese, onion powder and garlic powder; fold in noodles. Spread half of noodle mixture in a greased 2-quart casserole dish; top with half of beef mixture and half of cheese. Repeat layers. Bake, uncovered, at 350 degrees for 20 minutes, or until bubbly and cheese melts. Makes 8 servings.

Stack ribbon-tied bundles of sweet-scented candles in a basket near the front door...a pretty decoration that can double as gifts for surprise visitors.

Home for the Holidays

Aunt Barb's Pizza Casserole

Renae Scheiderer
Beallsville, OH

*My aunt sent me this recipe when I was first married and I didn't
know too much about cooking. It's simple and yummy, and you can
add other ingredients that your family likes. Bow-tie pasta works well
instead of lasagna noodles.*

5 to 6 lasagna noodles, uncooked
15-oz. jar pizza sauce, divided
8-oz. pkg. shredded mozzarella
  cheese, divided

1/2 c. sliced pepperoni, cut into
  quarters and divided
4-oz. can sliced mushrooms,
  drained and divided

Cook noodles according to package directions; drain. In a greased
2-quart casserole dish, layer half each of noodles, cutting to fit as
needed, and remaining ingredients. Repeat layers. Bake, uncovered, at
350 degrees for about 45 minutes, until hot and bubbly. Serves 4 to 6.

Stick-to-Your-Ribs Cube Steaks

Amanda Johnson
Marysville, OH

*This is one of my husband's favorite recipes...I am always happy
to make it for him! Serve with mashed potatoes and steamed
green beans for a complete, delicious meal.*

4 beef cube steaks
garlic powder, salt and pepper
  to taste

2 c. Worcestershire sauce
4 white onions, sliced

Sprinkle cube steaks with seasonings as desired; arrange steaks in a
greased deep 13"x9" baking pan. Pour Worcestershire sauce over steaks;
top with onions. Bake, uncovered, at 375 degrees for 30 to 40 minutes,
until steaks are fork-tender. Serves 4.

God bless us, every one!
– Charles Dickens

Cozy Christmas
COMFORTS

Sausage, Kale & Potato Casserole
Mary Bettuchy
Saint Robert, MO

This is my go-to recipe whenever I'm planning ahead for a busy week. The leftovers are just as good as when it first comes out of the oven, so I know we won't mind eating it again if I don't have time to cook! I like to use turkey kielbasa and 2% milk shredded cheese for a little less fat.

4 lbs. russet potatoes, peeled,
   and cut into chunks
1 T. salt
1/4 c. butter, sliced
3/4 c. milk
1 T. olive oil
1 onion, halved and thinly sliced
1 clove garlic, minced
1/2 c. cider vinegar
1/2 c. water
2 bunches fresh kale, coarsely
   chopped and stems trimmed
3/4 lb. Kielbasa or smoked pork
   sausage, sliced 1/2-inch thick
8-oz. pkg. shredded Monterey
   Jack or Cheddar cheese

In a large pot over high heat, cook potatoes in boiling water for 20 to 30 minutes, until tender; drain. Add salt and butter; mash until butter is well mixed. Add milk; continue to mash until creamy and smooth, adding more milk if needed. Set aside. Meanwhile, in a large stockpot, heat oil over medium-high heat until shimmering. Add onion and sauté for about 5 minutes, until translucent. Add garlic; cook one minute more. Add vinegar, water and kale; reduce heat to medium. Cover and cook for 10 to 15 minutes, stirring occasionally, until kale is wilted and soft. Spread mashed potatoes in the bottom of a greased 3-quart casserole dish; spread kale mixture over potatoes. Top with sausage slices. Bake, uncovered, at 350 degrees for 30 minutes, or until heated through and sausage is lightly golden. Sprinkle with cheese; bake 5 minutes more, or until cheese is melted. Serves 6 to 8.

Easily remove the tough stems from kale...fold each leaf in half, then cut down the side of the leaf the stem is on.

Pork Chops in Mushroom & Onion Gravy

Linda Diepholz
Lakeville, MN

I have been making this dish for years with just the onion, and started adding mushrooms as well for the last few years. It has great flavor and is very simple to make.

1 lb. boneless pork loin chops
2 c. onions, chopped
1 c. sliced mushrooms
1 c. reduced-sodium beef broth
1/4 t. pepper
1/3 c. milk
2 T. all-purpose flour

Spray a skillet with non-stick vegetable spray; heat over medium-high heat. Add pork chops and brown for about 5 minutes, turning once. Remove pork chops to a plate; cover to keep warm. Reduce heat to medium. Add onions and mushrooms to skillet; cook for 3 minutes. Stir in beef broth and pepper; return pork chops to skillet. Spoon onion mixture over pork chops. Cover and simmer over medium heat for 10 minutes, or until pork is no longer pink. In a cup, stir together milk and flour; add to skillet. Cook for 2 to 3 minutes, stirring constantly, until gravy is thickened. Serves 4.

A fragrant, spicy table accent...press whole cloves into the surface of a pillar candle to form a pattern.

Greek Baked Tilapia

Diana Migliaccio
Clifton, NJ

*This recipe is tasty and fast to prepare. Served with a tossed salad,
it's a great light meal when you've overindulged in holiday fare.*

1 lb. tilapia fillets, or other
    white fish
1/3 to 1/2 c. extra-virgin olive oil
salt and pepper to taste
2 c. bread, coarsely chopped into
    crumbs, or panko crumbs
1/2 c. fresh parsley, chopped
1/2 c. Kalamata olives, chopped

1/4 c. onion, finely chopped
1 roasted red pepper, patted dry
    and chopped
1 t. dried oregano
1/2 t. chili powder
1/3 to 1/2 c. crumbled feta
    cheese

Arrange fish fillets in a lightly greased 13"x9" baking pan. Drizzle lightly
with some of the olive oil; season with salt and pepper. In a bowl,
combine remaining ingredients except cheese. Drizzle with enough of
remaining oil to coat lightly. Spoon topping over and around fish;
sprinkle cheese over crumb layer. Bake, uncovered, at 350 degrees for
20 to 25 minutes, until golden. Serves 2 to 4.

Keep rolls warm alongside servings of soup. Before arranging rolls
in a bread basket, place a terra-cotta warming tile in the bottom
and line with a Christmasy tea towel.

Christmas Eve Fish

Brenda Bodnar
Mayfield Village, OH

On Christmas Eve, we have always enjoyed a simple dinner of this crumb-coated fish, coleslaw and French fries. A few years ago, my daughter and I started prepping the fish with my dad, now 89, so we could carry on the tradition.

3 lbs. orange roughy or
  sole fillets, thawed
2-1/2 c. all-purpose flour
2 t. salt
1 t. pepper
4 to 5 eggs, beaten

4 to 6 c. Italian-seasoned dry
  bread crumbs
canola oil for frying
Garnish: lemon slices,
  tartar sauce

Cut fish fillets into pieces about 4 inches square; pat dry. Set up 3 shallow bowls: one with flour, salt and pepper, one with beaten eggs and one with bread crumbs. Dredge each piece of fish in flour mixture, then in egg, then in bread crumbs, pressing crumbs to fish to coat well. Layer fish on wax paper-covered trays; set aside. Heat one inch of oil in a large cast-iron or stainless steel skillet. Working in batches, add 4 to 5 pieces of fish at a time; cook for about 5 minutes per batch, turning once, until deeply golden. Drain on paper-towel lined baking sheets; place in a 250-degree oven to keep warm. Serve with lemon slices and tartar sauce. Serves 6 to 8.

The best of all gifts around any Christmas tree...the presence of a happy family, all wrapped up in each other.
– Burton Hillis

Angel Hair Pasta with Tomato & Basil

JoAnn
Gooseberry Patch

This skillet recipe is so easy to put together! It's a delicious meatless main or side dish.

8-oz. pkg. angel hair pasta, uncooked
1 T. olive oil
2 cloves garlic, minced
1/4 c. sliced green onions
14-1/2 oz. can petite diced tomatoes

2 T. fresh basil, chopped
1 t. salt
1/4 t. pepper
Garnish: grated Parmesan cheese

Cook pasta according to package directions; drain. Meanwhile, heat oil in a large skillet; stir-fry garlic and onions for one minute. Add tomatoes with juice, basil, salt and pepper; cook and stir for 2 minutes. Add cooked pasta to skillet; toss to coat well. Serve topped with Parmesan cheese. Serves 6.

Creamy Pasta Florentine

Jen Thomas
Santa Rosa, CA

We enjoy this creamy, cheesy dish with grilled chicken or fish.

12-oz. pkg. fettuccine pasta, uncooked
10-oz. pkg. frozen chopped spinach, thawed
1 c. boiling water

2 to 3 cubes chicken bouillon
2/3 c. cream cheese, cubed
1/8 t. nutmeg
Optional: toasted bread crumbs, grated Parmesan cheese

Cook pasta according to package directions; add spinach to water during last 4 minutes of cooking time. Drain pasta and spinach. In a small saucepan over medium heat, combine water and bouillon until dissolved. Add cream cheese and nutmeg; cook and stir melted. Add to pasta mixture; toss to mix well. Garnish as desired. Serves 6.

Best Baked Ziti

Trudy Satterwhite
San Antonio, TX

This is a family favorite...warm and comforting,
yet simple to make.

16-oz. pkg. ziti pasta, uncooked
1 lb. ground beef
1 lb. ground sweet Italian pork
  sausage
1 onion, chopped
2 32-oz. jars spaghetti sauce

1 lb. provolone cheese, sliced
  and divided
1 c. sour cream, divided
1-1/2 c. shredded mozzarella
  cheese

Cook pasta according to package directions, just until tender; drain.
Meanwhile, brown beef, sausage and onion in a large skillet over
medium heat; drain. Stir in spaghetti sauce; reduce heat to low and
simmer for 15 minutes. In a lightly greased 13"x9" baking pan, layer
half each of pasta, provolone cheese, sour cream and sauce mixture.
Repeat layers; top with mozzarella cheese. Cover and bake at
350 degrees for 30 minutes, or until heated through and cheese
is melted. Makes 6 to 8 servings.

Make it easy on yourself when planning holiday dinners...stick to
tried & true recipes! You'll find your guests are just as happy with
simple comfort foods as with the most elegant gourmet meal.

Mom's Goulash

Dianna Oakland
Titusville, FL

My mom used to make this when were kids. I have tried so many versions of this recipe and never found the right combination until now. I know she's smiling in heaven when I make it!

1 lb. ground beef
1/2 c. onion, finely chopped
1/2 c. green pepper, finely chopped
3 stalks celery, finely chopped
1 clove garlic, minced
1 T. Worcestershire sauce
1 bay leaf
1 t. dried oregano
1/2 t. dried basil

salt and pepper to taste
15-oz. can diced tomatoes
8-oz. can tomato sauce
1 c. water
6-oz. can tomato paste
1 c. bowtie pasta, uncooked
3/4 c. shredded mozzarella cheese
1/4 c. grated Parmesan cheese

Brown beef in a large deep skillet over medium heat; drain. Stir in onion, green pepper, celery, garlic and Worcestershire sauce; add seasonings. Cook until vegetables are tender. Stir in tomatoes with juice, tomato sauce and water; reduce heat to low. Cover and cook for 20 minutes, stirring occasionally. Stir in tomato paste and uncooked pasta. Cook until pasta is tender, about 10 minutes. Discard bay leaf before serving. Top with cheese. Makes 6 to 8 servings.

A sweet placecard friends can take home. Write each friend's name on a vintage Christmas postcard, then clip onto the side of a plate.

Chicken & Wild Rice Casserole

Phyl Broich-Wessling
Garner, IA

Here is a real comfort-food casserole. I especially enjoy it on a cold winter day like today, with 6 to 12 inches of snow predicted for our area and strong winds to blow around that snow.

2 6-oz. pkgs. long-grain and
  wild rice, uncooked
3 lbs. boneless, skinless chicken
  breasts
1 c. chicken broth
1/2 c. dry sherry or chicken broth
1 c. celery, chopped
1 c. sweet or white onion,
  chopped
1 t. curry powder

1/2 t. kosher salt
1-1/2 T. butter
1 lb. sliced mushrooms
10-3/4 oz. can cream of
  mushroom soup
1 c. sour cream
1-1/2 c. shredded Italian-blend
  cheese, divided
1/2 c. sliced almonds, toasted
Garnish: chopped fresh parsley

Prepare rice according to package directions; cover and remove from heat. Meanwhile, in a large skillet, combine chicken, chicken broth, sherry or broth, celery, onion and seasonings. Bring to a boil over medium heat; cook for 7 to 10 minutes. Turn chicken over. Reduce heat to low and simmer for 45 minutes, or until chicken juices run clear. Remove from heat. Remove chicken to a plate; cool and cut into bite-size pieces. Drain skillet; add butter and mushrooms. Cook over medium heat, just until mushrooms are tender; drain and set aside. In a large bowl, combine chicken, mushrooms, cooked rice, soup, sour cream and one cup cheese. Stir gently; spoon into a lightly greased 13"x9" baking pan. Cover and bake at 350 degrees for 40 minutes. Uncover; top with almonds and remaining cheese. Bake for another 5 minutes, or until cheese is melted. Garnish with parsley before serving. Serves 6 to 8.

Toasting adds so much flavor to nuts. Spread nuts in a shallow pan in a single layer. Bake at 350 degrees for 4 to 6 minutes, until toasted, stirring halfway through.

Vegetable Medley Pot Roast

Mel Chencharick
Julian, PA

Winters in Pennsylvania can be downright bitter! Cold, windy and snowy...often it's a stay-at-home kind of day. This recipe is a great way to warm everyone through & through. Any leftover roast beef can be saved for a delicious sandwich another day.

3 to 4-lb. beef sirloin roast
1 T. kosher salt
1 T. pepper
1 c. beef broth
6 cloves garlic, peeled

1 lb. baby carrots
1 lb. fingerling potatoes,
   cut in half
1 yellow onion, cut into 8 wedges

Season roast with salt and pepper; place in a 6-quart slow cooker. Add beef broth; tuck garlic cloves around roast. Cover and cook on low setting for 6 hours. Arrange vegetables around roast; cover and cook on low setting for another 2 hours, or until tender. Serves 6.

Take the family to a local tree farm and cut your own
Christmas tree! Afterwards, warm up with mugs of hot cocoa.
You'll be creating sweet memories together.

Balsamic Roast Chicken

Ann Heavey
Bridgewater, MA

This is a recipe I have served many times to rave reviews.
It's great for a family Sunday dinner or for holiday guests.

5 to 6-lb. roasting chicken
1/4 c. fresh rosemary, chopped
4 cloves garlic, chopped
1 T. sea salt

1-1/2 t. pepper
1 red onion, chopped
2/3 c. balsamic vinegar
2/3 c. red wine or chicken broth

Pat chicken dry; set aside. In a small bowl, combine rosemary, garlic, salt and pepper. Rub mixture all over chicken, both inside and out. Let chicken stand for 30 minutes to one hour, or cover and refrigerate up to one day in advance to allow flavors to really blend. Arrange onion in the bottom of an ungreased roasting pan; place chicken on top of onion. Drizzle vinegar and wine or broth over chicken. Bake, uncovered, at 350 degrees for 2 to 2-1/2 hours, depending on size of chicken, until a meat thermometer inserted in thickest part reads 165 degrees. If chicken browns too quickly, cover with aluminum foil. Remove chicken to a serving platter. Slice and serve with sauce from pan. Serves 6.

Candied cranberries are a lovely garnish for roast chicken. In a saucepan, bring one cup water and one cup sugar almost to a boil, stirring until sugar dissolves. Pour into a bowl and add one cup fresh cranberries. Chill overnight; drain well. Toss cranberries with superfine sugar to coat and dry on wax paper.

Cozy Christmas
COMFORTS

Pasta Primavera Casserole

Liz Plotnick-Snay
Gooseberry Patch

Perfect for a holiday buffet...vegetarians will feel right
at home, and everyone else will enjoy it too.

16-oz. pkg. rigatoni pasta,
   uncooked
2 zucchini, cut into strips
2 red peppers, cut into strips
2 c. sliced mushrooms
1 c. green onions, chopped
1/3 c. butter
14-1/2 oz. can petite diced
   tomatoes

1/2 c. all-purpose flour
2 c. milk
2 c. vegetable broth
1/2 t. nutmeg
1/4 t. pepper
2 10-oz. pkgs. frozen chopped
   spinach, thawed and well
   drained

Cook pasta according to package directions; drain. Transfer pasta to a
greased deep 13"x9" baking pan; set aside. Meanwhile, melt butter in a
large skillet over medium heat. Sauté zucchini, red peppers, mushrooms
and onions for 3 to 4 minutes. Do not drain. Stir in tomatoes with juice;
spoon mixture over pasta. Sprinkle flour over skillet; blend in milk. Cook
and stir over medium heat until thickened. Stir in spinach; spoon over
pasta mixture. Cover and bake at 350 degrees for 40 to 45 minutes,
until hot and bubbly. Makes 8 servings.

Favorite Cheesy Bread

Catherine Snyder
Blue Springs, MO

This is my family's favorite accompaniment with pasta dishes.
We also enjoy it with soups and stews. Easy yet delicious!

1 large loaf Italian bread, sliced
   1-1/2 inches thick
2 c. mayonnaise

1 c. butter, softened
8-oz. pkg. shredded mozzarella
   cheese

Place bread slices cut-side down on ungreased baking sheets. Combine
mayonnaise and butter in a bowl; stir in cheese. Spread mixture evenly
over bread slices. Bake at 375 degrees for 12 to 15 minutes, until lightly
toasted and cheese is melted. Serves 8.

Home for the Holidays

Spinach-Artichoke Pasta

Jennifer Cole
Oxford, GA

This recipe combines so many yummy flavors, you just want to eat more. It tastes even better the next day! It's a great meatless main dish, or add some cooked chicken or shrimp for a heartier dish.

12-oz. pkg. penne pasta,
  uncooked
10-oz. pkg. frozen chopped
  spinach, thawed and very
  well drained
6-oz. jar artichoke hearts,
  drained and chopped

15-oz. jar Alfredo sauce
8-oz. pkg. shredded mozzarella
  cheese, divided
1 c. dry bread crumbs

Cook pasta according to package directions; drain and transfer to a large bowl. Add spinach, artichokes, Alfredo sauce and one cup cheese; mix thoroughly. Transfer to a greased 13"x9" baking pan. Sprinkle remaining cheese over top; sprinkle evenly with bread crumbs. Cover with aluminum foil. Bake at 350 degrees for 25 to 30 minutes, until cheese begins to bubble on top. Uncover; bake for an additional 5 minutes, until golden. Serves 6 to 8.

It's fun to hang little unexpected surprises from the dining room chandelier. Start with a swag of greenery, then tuck in Christmas whimsies like glass balls, tiny snowmen, cookie cutters and smiling Santas. So pretty...and a conversation piece at dinner!

Cozy Christmas
COMFORTS

Beef & Broccoli Stir-Fry

Linda Diepholz
Lakeville, MN

My family loves this recipe! It's quick & easy, so we enjoy it often.

1 lb. boneless beef top round
    or sirloin steak, cut into
    thin strips
2 T. oil, divided
4 c. broccoli, cut into bite-size
    flowerets
1/2 c. water

2 T. oyster sauce
1 T. soy sauce
1 T. cornstarch
1 t. sugar
cooked rice
Garnish: sliced green onions

Place beef strips in a large bowl; add Marinade. Stir to coat evenly.
Cover and refrigerate at least 30 minutes; discard ginger root. In a small
bowl, combine remaining ingredients except rice and garnish; set aside.
In a large skillet or wok, heat one tablespoon oil; add broccoli. Stir-fry
for 2 minutes, or until crisp-tender; remove from pan. Heat remaining
oil; add beef. Stir-fry for 5 minutes, or until browned. Add sauce mixture
to beef; cook and stir for 2 to 3 minutes, until thickened. Return broccoli
to pan; cook until heated through. Serve over cooked rice. Garnish with
a sprinkle of green onions. Serves 4 to 6.

Marinade:

1 T. cornstarch
1 T. oil
1 T. soy sauce

1 clove garlic, minced
3 to 4 slices fresh ginger root,
    peeled

Whisk together all ingredients.

Cut beef, chicken or pork into thin strips
or slices...easy! Just freeze for 20 to
30 minutes before slicing.

One-Pot Chinese Vegetable Casserole

*Koneta Bailey
Hillsboro, OH*

One of my family's favorites for many years...an easy one-pot dish that can be easily adapted for large or small gatherings. I like to serve it with hot buttered crescent rolls. Tastes great as leftovers too. This is an easy dish to fix ahead and warm up later, for a hearty hot meal in minutes.

1-1/2 lbs. lean ground beef
1 c. onion, diced
2 10-3/4 oz. cans golden
   mushroom soup
2 28-oz. cans chop suey
   vegetables, drained
Optional: 4-oz. can sliced
   mushrooms, drained

Optional: 8-oz. can sliced water
   chestnuts, drained
1 T. garlic, minced
2 c. instant rice, uncooked
4 cubes beef bouillon
3 c. water
pepper to taste
Garnish: soy sauce

In a large stockpot over medium heat, cook beef with onion until browned; drain. Add remaining ingredients. Cover and simmer over medium heat for 30 to 40 minutes, until heated through and rice is tender. May be simmered longer over low heat, to allow flavors to develop and sauce to thicken. Serve with soy sauce. Serves 10.

Tuck sweet family photos on wire picks into a festive evergreen arrangement. A super conversation starter for family & friends as they visit over the holidays.

Cozy Christmas
COMFORTS

Grandmama's Chicken & Dressing

Maranda Allen
Alexander City, AL

This is the recipe my granny (great-grandmother) made...my grandmother just simplified it some. It's a tradition for our Thanksgiving and Christmas every year. Everybody is always saying how wonderful it is!

13"x9" pan homemade cornbread
4 chicken breasts
12-oz. pkg. herb-seasoned
    stuffing mix
2 14-oz. cans chicken broth
10-3/4 oz. can cream of
    chicken soup

4 eggs, beaten
1 T. butter, softened
1 c. milk
1 to 2 c. celery, chopped
1/2 to 1 c. onion, chopped
1/2 to 1 c. green pepper, chopped

Cornbread may be made ahead of time. Crumble cornbread into bowl. In a saucepan, cover chicken with water; cook over medium-heat until tender. Cut chicken into cubes and add to bowl with cornbread. Add remaining ingredients; mix well, using a potato masher mash together. Mixture will be a little soupy. Transfer to a greased deep 13"x9" baking pan. Bake, uncovered, at 350 degrees for 30 minutes to one hour, until golden. Makes 20 servings.

Think of a few questions to ask during Christmas dinner. What's your Christmas wish this year? What's a favorite holiday memory? Do you have a New Year's goal? It's a nice way to share sweet memories and catch up with family & friends during this special time of year.

Home for the Holidays

Nancy's Chicken Delicious

Mary Scurti
Highland, CA

This is a favorite for family get-togethers and anytime I'm asked to bring a main-dish casserole to a party. I usually bring a copy of the recipe because someone always asks for it. Store-bought rotisserie chicken is a quick go-to for the chicken.

1/2 lb. sliced mushrooms
1-1/2 c. celery, finely chopped
3/4 c. onion, finely chopped
1/2 c. plus 2 T. butter, melted
  and divided
8-oz. can sliced water chestnuts,
  drained
1 c. mayonnaise

10-3/4 oz. can cream of
  mushroom soup
1/2 c. plus 2 T. milk
4 chicken breasts, cooked
  and diced
2 c. crumb-style cornbread
  stuffing, or 6-oz. pkg.
  cornbread stuffing

In a skillet over medium heat, sauté mushrooms, celery and onion in 2 tablespoons butter until tender. Stir in water chestnuts, mayonnaise, soup and milk; remove from heat. Spray a deep 13"x9" baking pan with non-stick vegetable spray. Spread chicken in pan; cover with soup mixture. Toss stuffing with remaining butter in a bowl; sprinkle on top. Bake, uncovered, at 350 degrees for 25 minutes, or until hot and bubbly. Serves 8 to 10.

For the sweetest family times, snuggle under a cozy throw and read favorite Christmas story books together. Young children will love being read to, while older kids may enjoy taking turns reading aloud from *"The Night Before Christmas"* or *"A Christmas Carol."*

Cozy Christmas
COMFORTS

Braised Pork Roast with Onion Gravy

Mary Thomason-Smith
Bloomington, IN

This recipe creates a fork-tender roast by braising slowly in flavorful seasoned broth. Surrounded with vegetables, it's a one-dish dinner.

3 T. Italian seasoning
1/4 t. red pepper flakes
1 t. salt
1/4 t. pepper
2-1/2 lb. pork loin roast
1 white onion, sliced

1 lb. baby carrots
4 redskin potatoes, quartered
1-1/2 c. beef broth
1 bay leaf
1 T. cold water
4 t. cornstarch

Mix together seasonings in a small bowl; sprinkle over all sides of roast. Place roast in a lightly greased 4-quart casserole dish; arrange vegetables around roast. Pour beef broth around roast and over vegetables; tuck in bay leaf. Cover tightly with aluminum foil; place casserole lid on top to create a tight seal. Bake at 325 degrees for 2-1/2 hours, or until a meat thermometer inserted in the center reads 145 degrees. Remove roast to a platter; cover and let stand for 15 minutes. Discard bay leaf. Pour pan juices into a saucepan; boil over medium-high heat for 10 to 12 minutes, until cooked down by half. In a small bowl, stir together water and cornstarch; add to juices. Cook and stir until thickened into gravy. Serve roast on a platter, surrounded by vegetables, with gravy on the side. Serves 4.

Herb butter is so versatile! Blend 1/2 cup softened butter and a teaspoon each of chopped fresh parsley, chives and dill. Form butter into a log on a piece of plastic wrap and freeze, or pack into a crock for a handy hostess gift.

Home for the Holidays

Aunt Minnie's Marmalade Pork Chops

Debrah Veronese
Bend, OR

*I spent all my summers growing up on my Aunt Minnie's farm.
I loved coming in from a day playing out in the fresh country air to
the smells of real country cooking. This was always my favorite!*

1 c. pure maple syrup
1 c. brown sugar, packed
2-1/2 c. apple cider or juice
1 c. raisins
1 c. sweetened dried cranberries

1 c. orange or citrus marmalade
6 country-style pork chops,
   thick-cut
2 t. granulated garlic

In a saucepan over medium heat, stir together maple syrup and brown
sugar; bring to a low boil. Stir in apple juice, raisins and cranberries;
simmer until fruit is soft. Stir in marmalade; cook until simmering.
Meanwhile, sprinkle pork chops with garlic; arrange in a lightly greased
13"x9" glass baking pan in a single layer. Spoon half of marmalade
mixture over pork chops. Bake, uncovered, at 325 degrees for
30 minutes. Remove from oven; spoon rest of marmalade mixture over
pork chops, reserving 1/2 cup in a small bowl. Bake an additional
10 to 15 minutes, until pork chops are done. Serve pork chops with
reserved warm marmalade mixture on the side. Makes 6 servings.

Sausage & Green Bean Dinner

Debra Mott
Mount Olive, IL

*This slow-cooker recipe has been a family favorite ever since
my kids were young...always requested!*

1 lb. Kielbasa sausage, sliced
4 to 6 potatoes, peeled, cubed
   and cooked

14-1/2 oz. can cut green beans
salt and pepper to taste

Layer sausage, potatoes and undrained beans in a 5-quart slow cooker;
sprinkle with seasonings. Cover and cook on low setting for 4 hours.
Makes 4 servings.

Mediterranean Party Rice

*Jacqueline Carucci
Hawthorne, NJ*

*Whenever we have a special occasion like a holiday or birthday,
I make this dish for my family and they gobble it up! So easy
and delicious...easily doubled for a crowd.*

2 T. butter, divided
1/2 lb. ground beef
1/2 lb. ground pork
1-1/2 t. allspice, or to taste
1-1/2 t. cinnamon
1-1/2 t. nutmeg

1 c. long-cooking rice, uncooked
2-1/4 c. low-sodium chicken
  broth
1/2 c. pine nuts
1/2 c. slivered almonds

Spray a large saucepan with non-stick vegetable spray. Melt one
tablespoon butter in pan over medium heat. Add beef and pork; cook for
6 to 9 minutes, until browned, breaking into small pieces with a spatula.
Drain; stir in spices, uncooked rice and chicken broth. Bring to a boil
over medium heat; reduce heat to medium-low. Cover and cook for
11 minutes, turning down heat a little more if mixture starts to smoke.
Remove from heat. Add remaining butter; cover and let stand for
5 minutes. Add pine nuts and almonds to a skillet over low heat; cook
and stir for one to 2 minutes, until toasted. Remove from heat and let
stand for 5 minutes. Add nuts to rice mixture; fluff rice with a fork and
serve. Serves 4 to 5.

Need a gift in a jiffy for a teacher, a neighbor or a friend with
a new baby? Give a loaf of freshly baked quick bread wrapped
in a pretty tea towel...it's sure to be appreciated.

Home for the *Holidays*

Spinach & Feta Turnovers

Robin Lazaro
Garner, NC

This is a family favorite I've perfected over the years. Everyone loves these turnovers, and they're easy to make

2 T. olive oil
1/4 c. onion, chopped
1 to 2 cloves garlic, minced
10-oz. pkg. frozen spinach,
   thawed and well drained
1/4 c. sour cream
1/8 t. nutmeg

salt and pepper to taste
1/2 c. crumbled feta cheese
Optional: 1/2 c. cooked chicken,
   shredded
8-oz. tube refrigerated crescent
   rolls
1 egg white, beaten

Heat olive oil in a skillet over medium heat. Add onion and garlic; cook and stir until translucent. Stir in spinach, sour cream and seasonings; remove from heat. Add cheese and chicken, if using; set aside. Separate crescent rolls, leaving each 2 triangles attached to form 4 squares. Press perforations to seal. Add 2 tablespoons spinach mixture to one half of each square. Fold over; seal edges with a fork. Place turnovers on an ungreased baking sheet. Bake at 350 degrees for 20 to 30 minutes, until golden. Makes 4 servings.

Dress up a stack of plain white gift bags with pom-pom snowman faces and fabric scrap scarves. A hot glue gun pulls it all together in just a few minutes. Tuck in tissue paper and gifts...now, aren't you clever!

Cozy Christmas
COMFORTS

Salmon au Gratin

Shirley Howie
Foxboro, MA

With the busy holiday season ahead, I like to have a few reliable one-dish recipes that are quick & easy to prepare. This tasty casserole fits the bill!

1 c. elbow macaroni, uncooked
1/2 c. onion, chopped
1/4 c. green pepper, chopped
2 T. butter
10-3/4 oz. can cream of celery soup
1/3 c. milk

1 t. mustard
1-1/2 c. shredded Cheddar cheese
14-3/4 oz. can salmon, drained and flaked
10-oz. pkg. frozen peas, thawed
1/4 c. grated Parmesan cheese

Cook macaroni according to package directions; drain. Meanwhile, in a skillet over medium heat, sauté onion and green pepper in butter until tender. Add soup, milk and mustard; stir until well blended. Spoon mixture into a greased 2-quart casserole dish. Add cooked macaroni, Cheddar cheese, salmon and peas; stir well. Top with Parmesan cheese. Bake, uncovered, at 350 degrees for 30 to 35 minutes, until heated through. Serves 4.

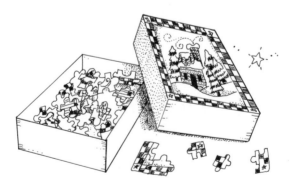

Start a new tradition! Lay out a Christmas-themed jigsaw puzzle early in December. Family members are sure to enjoy fitting a few pieces in place whenever they pass by.

Eggplant Parmigiana

Nancy Christensen
West Des Moines, IA

*I've been making this recipe since 2002, so you know it's
a keeper! It's a meatless main everyone can enjoy.*

3/4 lb. eggplant, peeled and cut
   crosswise into 1/2-inch slices
1 egg, beaten
1/4 c. all-purpose flour

2 T. oil
1/3 c. shredded Parmesan cheese
1 c. meatless spaghetti sauce
1 c. shredded mozzarella cheese

Dip eggplant slices into egg, then into flour, turning to coat both sides.
Heat oil in a large skillet over medium heat. Add half of eggplant and
cook for 4 to 6 minutes, until golden, turning once. Drain on paper
towels; repeat with remaining eggplant. Arrange eggplant in a single
layer in a greased 2-quart casserole dish. Sprinkle with Parmesan
cheese; top with sauce and mozzarella cheese. Bake, uncovered, at
400 degrees for 10 to 12 minutes, until heated through. Serves 4.

Crazy-Good Popovers

Amy Thomason Hunt
Traphill, NC

*These little popovers are excellent with just about any meal
you choose. They're even good as an appetizer or snack!*

2 c. biscuit baking mix
2/3 c. milk
1/2 c. shredded Cheddar cheese
4 green onions, chopped

8 slices bacon, crisply cooked
   and crumbled
2 T. butter, melted

In a large bowl, combine all ingredients except butter. Mix thoroughly
until a soft dough forms. Drop dough by tablespoonfuls onto a baking
sheet sprayed with non-stick vegetable spray. Bake at 450 degrees for
7 to 9 minutes, until golden. Brush with melted butter; serve warm.
Makes about one dozen.

Cozy Christmas
COMFORTS

Company's Coming Chicken

Michelle Powell
Valley, AL

So delicious and impressive...but no one guesses
how easy this is!

1/4 c. milk	1 c. whipping cream
1/4 c. dry bread crumbs	4-oz. jar sliced pimentos, drained
4 boneless, skinless chicken	1/2 c. grated Parmesan cheese
breasts	2 T. dried basil
3 T. butter	1/8 t. pepper
1/2 c. chicken broth	cooked egg noodles

Place milk and bread crumbs in separate shallow bowls. Dip chicken
into milk; coat in crumbs. Melt butter in a skillet over medium-high
heat. Cook chicken on both sides until juices run clear. Remove to a
plate; keep warm. Add chicken broth to skillet juices in skillet. Bring to
a boil, stirring to loosen browned bits from the pan. Stir in cream and
pimentos. Boil and stir for one minute. Reduce heat to medium-low.
Add cheese, basil and pepper. Cook and stir until heated through. To
serve, place chicken on egg noodles; spoon sauce from skillet over
chicken. Makes 4 servings.

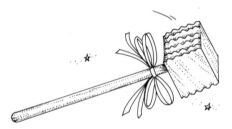

Boneless chicken breasts cook up quickly and evenly when flattened...
they're more elegant on a dinner plate, too! Simply place chicken
between 2 pieces of plastic wrap and gently pound to desired
thickness with a meat mallet.

Home for the Holidays

One-Pot Pork Chop Dinner

Diana Spray
Medora, IN

A favorite of my family...it's a whole meal in the slow cooker.

6 pork chops, 3/4-inch thick
1 T. oil
1 onion, sliced
1 green pepper, chopped
4-oz. can mushroom stems & pieces, drained

8-oz. can tomato sauce
1 T. brown sugar, packed
2 t. Worcestershire sauce
1-1/2 t. cider vinegar
1/2 t. salt
cooked rice

In a skillet over medium heat, brown pork chops in oil on both sides; drain. Transfer pork chops to a 6-quart slow cooker; add onion, green pepper and mushrooms. In a bowl, combine remaining ingredients except rice. Spoon over pork chops and vegetables. Cover and cook on low setting for 4 to 5 hours, until pork chops are tender. Serve over cooked rice. Makes 6 servings.

For old-fashioned farmhouse charm, group together an assortment of vintage tin graters on a tabletop or mantel. Tuck a tea light under each and enjoy their cozy flickering lights.

Cozy Christmas
COMFORTS

Tourtière

Tammy Griffin
Ontario, Canada

My house would not be Christmas without the pleasant aroma of a delicious Tourtière baking in the oven. It always reminds me of my grandmother's house when we came home from Midnight Mass.

3/4 lb. ground pork
3/4 lb. ground beef
1 T. butter
3/4 c. onion, chopped
2 c. beef broth

1/4 t. cinnamon
1 bay leaf
1 t. coarse salt
pepper to taste
2 9-inch pie crusts, unbaked

In a large, heavy saucepan over medium heat, cook pork and beef until no longer pink. Drain and set aside. Melt butter in saucepan; add onion and sauté until soft. Return pork mixture to pan; stir in beef broth and seasonings. Reduce heat to medium-low. Cover and simmer gently for 2 to 2-1/2 hours. Discard bay leaf. Line a 9" pie plate with one pie crust; fill with pork mixture. Cover with top crust; trim crust, crimp edges to seal and cut steam vents. Bake at 400 degrees for 15 minutes. Lower oven temperature to 350 degrees; bake another 20 to 30 minutes, until crust is lightly golden. Makes 8 servings.

When choosing candles for the dinner table, consider how well the scent will go with food. Natural beeswax candles have an appealing mild scent...their warm amber color enhances any harvest table too.

Upper-Crust Chicken

Sandy Coffey
Cincinnati, OH

An easy recipe for meals during gift-wrap or trim-a-tree sessions. Serve with hot rolls and a tossed salad for an easy and delicious dinner.

8 slices bread
2 c. cooked chicken, cubed
1 c. celery, chopped
2 c. shredded Cheddar cheese,
 divided

2 eggs, beaten
1 c. mayonnaise
1/2 t. poultry seasoning
1/2 t. salt
2 c. milk

Trim crusts from bread; cut crusts into small cubes. In a bowl, combine crusts, chicken, celery and 1-3/4 cups cheese. Spoon mixture into a greased 13"x9" baking pan. Cut bread slices into quarters; arrange on top of mixture and set aside. In a separate bowl, whisk together eggs, mayonnaise and seasonings. Gradually add milk, mixing well. Pour over top. Sprinkle with remaining cheese. Cover and refrigerate for several hours. Bake, uncovered, at 375 degrees for 30 to 40 minutes, until puffed and golden. Makes 6 servings.

We wish you a Merry Christmas,
We wish you a Merry Christmas,
We wish you a Merry Christmas,
And a Happy New Year.
– Traditional carol

Cozy Christmas
COMFORTS

Party-Perfect Pulled Pork

Penny Sherman
Ava, MO

This is my go-to slow-cooker recipe all fall and winter for football parties, holiday parties, you name it! It's so easy, yet feeds a crowd. Just add chips and coleslaw.

1-1/2 t. smoked paprika
1 t. cayenne pepper
1 t. dried thyme
1 t. garlic powder
1/2 t. salt
2 t. pepper

5-lb. boneless pork shoulder
   roast
1 c. water
16 to 20 sandwich buns, split
Garnish: favorite barbecue sauce

Combine all seasonings in a small bowl; rub evenly over all sides of roast. Add roast to a 6-quart slow cooker; add water. Cover and cook on low setting for 6 to 8 hours, or on high setting for 4 to 5 hours, until roast is very tender. Remove roast to a platter; let stand for 10 to 15 minutes. Shred with 2 forks. Serve pork in buns, topped with barbecue sauce. Makes 16 to 20 servings.

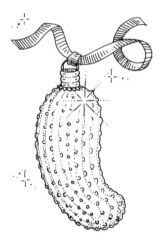

Start a new tradition...hide a glass pickle ornament among the branches of a decorated tree. When it's time to pack away the decorations, whoever finds the pickle gets just one more surprise!

Home for the **Holidays**

1-2-3 Italian Beef

Joyce Teague
Providence, KY

This slow-cooker recipe is so easy that anyone can make it! It is absolutely delicious after a cold day of Christmas gift shopping... perfect for Christmas get-togethers too.

5 to 6-lb. beef chuck roast
3 T. oil
2 16-oz. jars pepperoncini
    peppers

10 to 12 buns, split

In a large pan over medium heat, brown roast in oil on all sides. Place roast in a 6-quart slow cooker; cover with peppers, juice and all. Cover and cook on low setting for 9 to 10 hours, or on high setting for 5 to 6 hours. Shred with 2 forks; serve on buns. Makes 10 to 12 servings.

Shredded Italian Chicken

Lori Simmons
Princeville, IL

A wonderful slow-cooker recipe...very tasty and flavorful. Can add a touch of BBQ sauce on top of your sandwich for a zesty taste. Serve with chips and a drink for a wonderful meal.

6 boneless, skinless chicken
    breasts
2 0.7-oz. pkgs. Italian salad
    dressing mix, divided

3 c. water, divided
Optional: barbecue sauce
8 sandwich buns

Place chicken in a 6-quart slow cooker; add one package salad dressing mix and 2 cups water. Cover and cook for 7 to 8 hours, until very tender. Shred chicken with a fork; stir in remaining dressing mix and additional water, if needed. Stir in barbecue sauce, if desired. Warm through on low setting. Serve on buns. Serves 6 to 8.

Toast sub buns before adding shredded beef, pork or chicken... such a tasty difference! Buns will drip less too.

177

Cozy Christmas
COMFORTS

Slow-Cooker Beef Tips

Ramona Storm
Gardner, IL

I've used this recipe for years! It goes together fast and smells great while it cooks. Good over cooked rice or mashed potatoes too.

1/4 c. all-purpose flour
1/8 t. seasoned salt
salt and pepper to taste
2 lbs. lean stew beef cubes
1/2 c. onion, coarsely chopped
4-oz. can sliced mushrooms,
   drained

14-oz. can beef broth
1 t. Worcestershire sauce
2 T. catsup
1/4 c. water
cooked egg noodles

Combine flour and seasonings in a large plastic zipping bag. Add beef cubes to bag; toss to coat well. Transfer beef to a 4-quart slow cooker. If any flour mixture is left, sprinkle it over beef. Layer onion and mushrooms over beef; set aside. In a bowl, whisk together remaining ingredients except noodles; pour over beef. Cover and cook on low setting for 8 hours. To serve, spoon beef mixture over cooked egg noodles. Serves 8.

Put together a savory dinner in your slow cooker, then enjoy some winter fun with your family. After ice skating or a hike in the snow, a hot, delicious meal will be waiting to warm you up...what could be cozier?

Home for the Holidays

Hawaiian Spareribs

Jen Stout
Blandon, PA

Looking for a new pork recipe for New Year's Day? This recipe is just a little different...sweet, savory and so easy to make.

3-1/2 to 4 lbs. pork spareribs, cut into serving-size portions
3 cloves garlic, pressed
salt and pepper to taste
1 onion, sliced
1/4 c. water
20-oz. can crushed pineapple
12-oz. bottle chili sauce
1/2 c. brown sugar, packed
1 t. ground ginger
1/2 t. dry mustard
cooked rice

Rub spareribs with garlic; season with salt and pepper. Arrange onion slices in a lightly greased roasting pan; place spareribs on top. Pour water into pan; cover with aluminum foil. Bake at 350 degrees for 30 minutes. In a bowl, combine undrained pineapple and remaining ingredients; spoon over spareribs. Bake, uncovered, one hour longer. Serve over cooked rice. Makes 4 to 6 servings.

Make mini wreaths of rosemary to slip around dinner napkins. Simply wind fresh rosemary stems into a ring shape, tuck in the ends and tie on a tiny bow...so festive!

Cozy Christmas
COMFORTS

Hoppin' John

Rebecca Turner
Dallas, TX

This recipe is great for a crowd on a cold day, and especially on New Year's Day...delish! Can be divided and frozen for multiple meals for smaller groups or couples. Serve over cooked rice with some warm cornbread on the side.

1 lb. ground pork sausage
1 lb. ground beef
2 bunches green onions, chopped
3 stalks celery, chopped
1/2 green pepper, chopped
1/2 red pepper, chopped

4 cloves garlic, minced
1 T. sugar
2 10-oz. cans diced tomatoes
  with green chiles
3 16-oz. cans black-eyed peas
cooked rice

In a large heavy stockpot, brown sausage and beef over medium heat; drain. Add remaining ingredients except rice; stir well. Reduce heat to medium-low. Cover and simmer for one hour, or until very thick, stirring occasionally. May also simmer longer over low heat. Serve over cooked rice. Makes 10 to 12 servings.

Setting the table with stemmed glasses? Open up colorful napkins, gather each in the middle and slip them, center down, into each glass...an instant dress-up for the table!

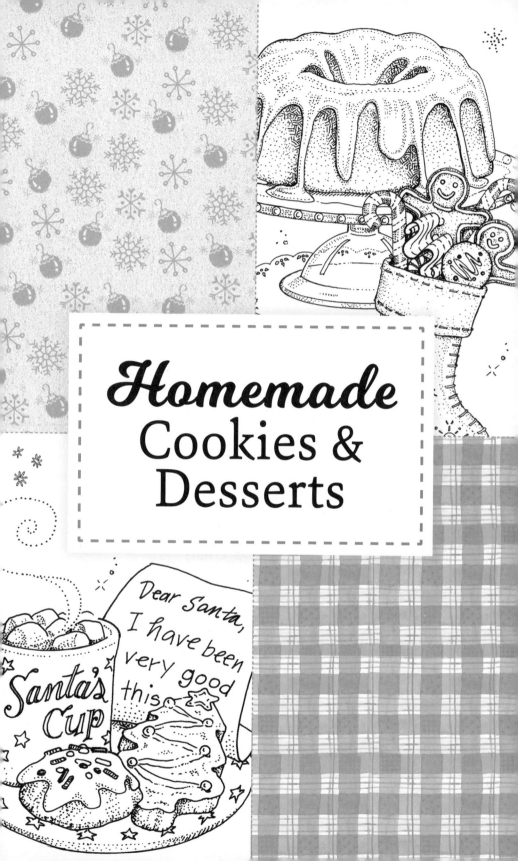

Homemade
Cookies &
Desserts

Cozy Christmas
COMFORTS

Grandma's Frosted Shortbread Cookies

Kandy Bingham
Green River, WY

This cookie recipe is from my grandma. My husband makes it every Christmas, using holiday-themed cookie cutters to cut out the cookies. He decorates the cookies with the Buttercream Frosting...they're wonderful for our cookie plates.

2 c. butter
2 c. powdered sugar
2 eggs, beaten
1 T. almond extract

2 t. vanilla extract
5 c. all-purpose flour, sifted
1/2 t. salt

In a large bowl, with an electric mixer fitted with a paddle, beat together butter, powdered sugar, eggs and extracts. Mix in flour, one cup at a time. Turn dough out onto a lightly floured surface and shape into a disc. Wrap with plastic wrap; chill for 30 minutes. On a lightly floured surface, roll dough to about 1/8-inch thickness. Cut into desired shapes using cookie cutters. Place on ungreased baking sheets. Bake at 375 degrees for 15 to 18 minutes. Cool cookies on a wire rack; frost with Buttercream Frosting. Makes 2 to 3 dozen.

Buttercream Frosting:

1/2 c. shortening
1/2 c. butter, softened
1 t. vanilla extract
4 c. powdered sugar

2 T. milk
Optional: several drops food
  coloring

Beat butter and shortening with an electric mixer on medium-low speed. Add vanilla. Gradually beat in powdered sugar. Add milk; beat until light and fluffy. Tint with food coloring, if desired.

Cut-out cookies will keep their shape better if chilled on the baking sheet before baking.

Homemade
Cookies & Desserts

Soft Coffee Cookies

Lisa Ludwig
Fort Wayne, IN

When I was a little girl, my mom would make these cookies for us long before I became a real fan of coffee. They were always so good as they came out of the oven, all warm and a little steamy, enjoyed with an ice-cold glass of milk. A fond childhood memory.

1 c. butter-flavored shortening
2 c. light brown sugar, packed
2 eggs, beaten
1/2 c. cold brewed coffee
3-1/2 c. all-purpose flour

1 t. baking soda
1 t. salt
1 t. nutmeg
1 t. cinnamon
Garnish: sugar

In a large bowl, blend together shortening, brown sugar and eggs. Add coffee and mix well. Add remaining ingredients except garnish; stir well. Cover and chill for at least one hour or overnight. Drop by teaspoonfuls onto ungreased baking sheets. Bake at 400 degrees for 8 to 10 minutes. Remove cookies to a wire rack; sprinkle with sugar while still warm. Makes 4 dozen.

Send a Christmas cookie party in a box! When wrapping up gift boxes of homebaked cookies, why not tuck in a package of paper holiday napkins and a box of spiced tea?

Cozy Christmas
COMFORTS

Cherry Pistachio Cookies

Lisa Zamfina
Fairfield, CT

These are not too sweet and will disappear quickly. The first time I made these cookies, I had to hide them from my husband. He found almost all of my hiding spots! I did end up with a plateful to share with family & friends at Christmas. I hope you will enjoy them too.

1 c. butter, room temperature
1/2 c. sugar
1/2 t. salt
1 egg, separated
2-1/4 c. all-purpose flour

1/2 c. pistachios, coarsely chopped
8-oz. container candied red cherries, coarsely chopped
1/3 c. coarse sugar

In a large bowl, with an electric mixer on medium speed, beat together butter, sugar and salt; beat in egg yolk. (Refrigerate egg white for later.) Add flour and pistachios; beat on low speed until just combined. Remove dough from mixer to a lightly floured surface. Using your hands, mix in cherries. Divide dough in half; roll each half into a log, about 12 inches long. Wrap in plastic and refrigerate overnight. Pour coarse sugar onto a long piece of parchment paper. Lightly brush egg white over the surface of each log; press and roll logs into sugar. Transfer logs to a cutting board; slice 1/2-inch thick. Place slices on parchment paper-lined baking sheets, one inch apart. Bake on center rack of oven at 350 degrees for 12 to 15 minutes. Cool cookies completely on wire racks. Store in an airtight container, or freeze for up to 2 weeks. Makes 4 dozen.

Early in the holiday season, make a list of cookies to bake, cards to send and gifts to buy...even Santa makes a list! Post it on the fridge, and you'll be able to check off each item with satisfaction as it's completed.

Homemade
Cookies & Desserts

Thumbprint Cookies

Hannah Cuffman
Roanoke, VA

These cookies are so small and delicate...everyone loves them!

1/4 c. brown sugar, packed
1/4 c. shortening
1/4 c. butter, softened
1 egg, separated
1/2 t. vanilla extract

1 c. all-purpose flour
1/4 t. salt
3/4 c. nuts, finely chopped
4 to 6 T. raspberry jam or other
    favorite jam

In a large bowl, blend brown sugar, shortening, butter, egg yolk and vanilla. Add flour and salt; mix until dough holds together. Shape dough into one-inch balls; set aside. Beat egg white lightly. Dip each dough ball into egg white until coated; roll in chopped nuts. Arrange dough balls on ungreased baking sheets, about one inch apart. Press your thumb deeply (but carefully) into the center of each dough ball to create an indentation. Bake at 350 degrees for 6 minutes, or until lightly golden. Cool. Fill each thumbprint with 1/2 teaspoon jam. Makes 2 to 3 dozen.

Search Grandma's recipe box for that extra-special cookie
you remember...and then bake some to share with the whole
family. If you don't have her recipe box, maybe you'll spot
a similar recipe in a Gooseberry Patch cookbook!

Cozy Christmas
COMFORTS

Gingerbread Crispy Rice Treats
Kathy Pusakulich
Ironwood, MI

*Whoever tries these loves them! They travel well. Gingerbread
pudding is seasonal...if you can't find it, give butterscotch a try.*

5 T. butter, softened and divided
10-oz. pkg. marshmallows
3.4-oz. pkg. instant gingerbread
    pudding mix
1 t. vanilla extract

4 c. crispy rice cereal
1-1/2 c. white chocolate chips,
    divided
5 gingersnap cookies, crushed

Line a 9"x9" baking pan with aluminum foil; grease with one tablespoon
butter and set aside. Add remaining butter to a large microwave-safe
bowl; microwave until melted. Add marshmallows; microwave until
melted. Stir well; fold in pudding mix and vanilla. Stir in cereal; coat
completely with marshmallow mixture. Stir in 3/4 cup chocolate chips.
Press mixture into pan. Microwave remaining chips in a separate bowl
until melted; spread over top. Sprinkle with crushed cookies. Cool
completely. Cut into squares; store in an airtight container. Makes
2 dozen.

Vianna's Cinnamon Twists
Cathy Doucet
Quebec, Canada

*My mother has been making these cookies since before I was born.
They are a very simple cookie, but one of my favorites. They bring
back warm memories of us baking in the kitchen together.*

3 eggs, beaten
1 c. sugar
3/4 c. oil
2 t. baking powder

3-1/2 c. all-purpose flour
Garnish: 1/2 c. sugar,
    1 t. cinnamon

In a large bowl, blend eggs, one cup sugar and oil. Stir in baking powder
and enough flour to make a soft dough. Roll pieces of dough into long
pencil-thick rolls; roll in cinnamon-sugar. Twist into figure 8's. Place
on lightly greased baking sheets. Bake at 375 degrees for 10 to
12 minutes, until golden. Makes 3 to 4 dozen.

Homemade Cookies & Desserts

Meringue Pecan Bars

Leona Krivda
Belle Vernon, PA

These are always one of the cookies I make at Christmas. I don't know why I don't make them more often! For the holidays, I make three batches, and they are gone in no time.

1/2 c. butter
1-3/4 c. brown sugar, packed
1 egg, separated
2 t. vanilla extract, divided
1-1/2 c. all-purpose flour
1 t. baking powder
1/2 c. chopped pecans
1/2 c. sweetened flaked coconut

In a large bowl, combine butter, 1/2 cup brown sugar, one egg yolk and one teaspoon vanilla; blend well. Sift together flour and baking powder; add to butter mixture and mix well. Press dough into an ungreased 9"x9" baking pan; set aside. In a separate bowl, with an electric mixer on high speed, beat one egg white until soft peaks form. Add remaining vanilla and remaining brown sugar; beat well until glossy. With a spoon, fold in nuts and coconut. Spread brown sugar mixture evenly over dough. Bake at 350 degrees for 25 minutes. Cut into bars while still warm. Makes 12 to 16 bars.

I plead for memories of olden times, and simple pleasures, and the making of the most delightful music in the world... the laughter of happy children. God bless us all and make us contented. Merry Christmas!

– A.M. Hopkins

Cozy Christmas
COMFORTS

Holiday Haystack Cookies

Ellen Folkman
Crystal Beach, FL

Years ago, I was looking for something different to include with my holiday cookie tins for family & friends. This was the perfect addition, and it's now a favorite! It's yummy and quick to make.

1-1/2 c. chow mein noodles
1-1/4 c. roasted peanuts
1/4 c. mini red and green
    candy-coated chocolates

10-oz. pkg. peanut butter chips
1 T. shortening

In a large bowl, combine noodles, peanuts and chocolates; mix well and set aside. In a microwave-safe bowl, combine peanut butter chips and shortening. Microwave on high for one to 2 minutes, stirring once, until almost melted. Remove from microwave; stir until smooth. For each cookie, spoon one teaspoon peanut butter mixture onto a wax paper-lined baking sheet; spread into a 2-inch circle with back of spoon. Heap one tablespoon noodle mixture onto circle. Drizzle with one teaspoon peanut butter mixture; sprinkle with one tablespoon noodle mixture. Chill for 15 minutes, or until peanut butter sets. Cover tightly and store in a cool area. Makes 2 dozen.

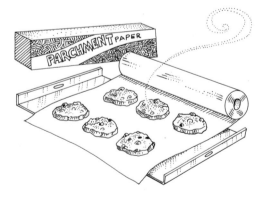

Parchment paper is a baker's best friend. Place it on a baking sheet to keep cookies from spreading and sticking. Clean-up is a breeze too...just toss away the paper! Look for rolls of parchment paper at the supermarket, next to the wax paper.

Homemade Cookies & Desserts

Chocolate Christmas Fudge

Trudy Satterwhite
San Antonio, TX

It wouldn't be Christmas without our Christmas fudge!

3/4 c. margarine
3 c. sugar
2/3 c. evaporated milk
12-oz. pkg. semi-sweet
   chocolate chips

7-oz. jar marshmallow creme
1 t. vanilla extract
Optional: 1 c. chopped pecans

Combine margarine, sugar and evaporated milk in a heavy 2-1/2 quart saucepan. Bring to a full rolling boil over medium heat, stirring constantly. Continue boiling for 4 minutes on medium heat, stirring constantly to prevent burning. Remove from heat. Gradually stir in chocolate chips until melted. Add remaining ingredients; mix well. Pour into a greased 13"x9" baking pan. Cool at room temperature; cut into squares. Makes 3 pounds.

Easy Peanut Butter Fudge

Linda Murray
Brentwood, NH

I've been making this recipe for years! Smooth and creamy, it tastes wonderful. It cooks up fast in the microwave and sets within the hour. I give it as gifts at Christmas.

1 c. creamy peanut butter
1 c. butter
1 t. vanilla extract

4 c. powdered sugar
Optional: 1 c. baking cocoa

Microwave peanut butter and butter in a microwave-safe container on high until fully melted; stir until smooth. Add vanilla, powdered sugar and cocoa, if using; stir until smooth. Pour into a wax paper-lined, buttered 8"x8" baking pan. Refrigerate until hardened. Cut with a sharp knife. Makes 3 dozen pieces.

Mmm...super-size fudge cups! Just spoon warm fudge into foil muffin cups. Wrap individually in squares of colorful cellophane.

Cozy Christmas COMFORTS

Cranberry Caramel Cake

Debbie Cutelli
Saint Louis, MO

This cake is great any time of the day. Who doesn't love pumpkin and cranberries during the holidays? The caramel sauce makes it extra special.

18-1/4 oz. pkg. yellow cake
   mix with pudding
4 eggs, beaten
1 c. eggnog
1/3 c. oil

2 t. pumpkin pie spice
1-1/2 c. fresh or frozen
   cranberries, chopped
1 c. chopped walnuts

In a large bowl, combine dry cake mix, eggs, eggnog, oil and spice. Beat with an electric mixer on low speed for 30 seconds; beat for 2 minutes on medium speed. Fold in cranberries and walnuts. Pour batter into a greased and lightly floured 12-cup fluted tube pan. Bake at 350 degrees for 45 to 55 minutes, until a toothpick inserted near center comes out clean. Cool in pan for 10 minutes. Invert cake onto a wire rack; remove pan and cool for about one hour. Drizzle warm Caramel Sauce over cake before serving. Makes 16 servings.

Caramel Sauce:

1/2 c. butter
1-1/4 c. brown sugar, packed

2 T. light corn syrup
1/2 c. whipping cream

Melt butter in a saucepan over medium-high heat. Stir in brown sugar and corn syrup; bring to a boil. Cook for one minute or until sugar dissolves, stirring constantly. Stir in cream. Return to a boil, stirring constantly. Remove from heat.

Candied red and green cherries, cut in half, make a pretty and quick garnish for a holiday Bundt® cake.

Homemade
Cookies & Desserts

Warm Winter Lemon Cake

Joyceann Dreibelbis
Wooster, OH

This warm dessert has it all! Luscious and lemony, molten and moist...pudding and cake! The lemon filling transforms from saucy and gooey to thick and custard-like.

18-1/4 oz. pkg. yellow cake mix
2 c. cold milk
1-1/4 c. water
2 3.4-oz. pkgs. instant lemon
    pudding mix

1/3 c. sugar
2 T. powdered sugar

Prepare cake mix according to package directions. Pour batter into a greased 13"x9" baking pan; set aside. Combine milk and water in a large bowl. Add dry pudding mixes and sugar. Whisk together for 2 minutes, or until well blended. Pour over batter in pan. Set pan on a baking sheet to catch drips; mixture will bubble. Bake at 350 degrees for 50 to 60 minutes, until a toothpick comes out clean. Cool in pan for 20 minutes. Sprinkle with powdered sugar; spoon into serving dishes. Serve warm. Makes 16 servings.

The golden glow of candlelight adds a magic touch to any gathering. For all the charm of real flames, use battery-operated candles and tealights...there's no need to worry about children or pets touching them.

Cozy Christmas
COMFORTS

Grandma Letha's Oatmeal Cookies

Cindy Whitney
Bar Mills, ME

My grandparents Ernie and Letha were a wonderful Mennonite couple who lived in Michigan. They were married for over 60 years. Grandma always made these delicious oatmeal cookies for family get-togethers...29 cousins and their parents (six sets of aunts & uncles!), family reunions in Michigan to fish in the pond, skate on the pond, play board games, sing, help in the gardens. So many holidays, so many memories, always Grandma's cookies!

6 c. old-fashioned oats,
   uncooked
4 c. all-purpose flour
2 c. sugar
2 c. brown sugar, packed
2 t. baking soda

2 t. salt
2 c. chopped walnuts
4 eggs, beaten
2 c. oil
2 t. vanilla extract

In a very large bowl, mix together oats, flour, sugars, baking soda, salt and walnuts; mix well. In a separate bowl, whisk together eggs, oil and vanilla; add to oat mixture and stir until combined. Form dough into long rolls, about 3 inches thick. Wrap in plastic wrap; freeze. To serve, slice 1/2-inch thick; place on ungreased baking sheets. Bake at 350 degrees for 10 minutes. Makes 6 dozen.

A nifty way to make perfectly shaped slice & bake cookies! Fill clean, empty small orange juice cans with dough and freeze. To bake, let thaw for 15 minutes, then remove the bottom of the can and push up the dough. Cut dough across open end of can...ready to bake!

Homemade
Cookies & Desserts

Gingerbread Cookies

Jan Abney
Salem, MO

*A great traditional holiday treat! Kids love to decorate them,
so set out some frosting and raisins.*

4 c. all-purpose flour
3/4 t. baking soda
1 t. salt
4 t. ground ginger
1 t. ground cloves
1 T. cinnamon

2/3 c. butter or coconut oil,
  melted and cooled
2/3 c. sugar
3 eggs, beaten
2/3 c. molasses
Optional: additional sugar

In a large bowl, combine flour, baking soda, salt and spices; mix well and set aside. In a separate bowl, blend butter or oil and sugar. Stir in eggs and molasses; add to flour mixture and mix well. Cover and chill dough for one hour. On a floured surface, roll out dough to 1/8-inch thick. With a cookie cutter, cut into gingerbread men. Arrange cookies on parchment paper-lined baking sheets. Sprinkle with sugar, if desired. Bake at 350 degrees for 7 to 10 minutes. Makes 3 dozen.

Bake up oodles of gingerbread people! Hanging from the tree, marching across a mantel or piled in a bowl, they add a little extra cheer to holiday decorating.

Cozy Christmas
COMFORTS

Rudolph's Nose Cookies

Crystal Branstrom
Russell, PA

This is a recipe that my friend Katey so graciously shared with me.
They are my favorite holiday cookies...Santa loves them too!

3/4 c. butter
1 c. sugar, divided
1 egg yolk, beaten
1 t. vanilla extract
1-1/2 c. all-purpose flour

1/4 c. baking cocoa
36 maraschino cherries, well
    drained
1/2 c. semi-sweet chocolate chips
1 t. shortening

In a large bowl, blend together butter, 1/2 cup sugar, egg yolk and vanilla; set aside. Sift together flour and cocoa; blend with butter mixture. Shape dough into one-inch balls; roll in remaining sugar. Place dough balls on ungreased baking sheets; make an indentation in each with your thumb. Bake at 375 degrees for 7 to 9 minutes. Cool on wire racks. Place Frosting in a piping bag with a large star tip; frost cookies. Place a cherry in the center of each cookie, pressing down lightly. In a microwave-safe bowl, microwave chocolate chips with shortening for 30 to 90 seconds, until melted. Drizzle chocolate over cookies. Makes 3 dozen.

Frosting:

1/4 c. butter
1/2 t. almond extract

1 c. powdered sugar

Blend together butter and extract. Add powdered sugar; beat until smooth and creamy.

To stir up frosting in the reddest red, the greenest green and other extra bright holiday colors, choose paste-style food coloring...a little goes a long way!

Homemade
Cookies & Desserts

Santa Claus Whiskers

Judy Lange
Imperial, PA

Cherries and coconut make these look so festive on a cookie tray!

1 c. butter, softened
1 c. sugar
2 T. milk
1 t. vanilla extract
2-1/2 c. all-purpose flour

1 c. candied red cherries, finely
   chopped
1/2 c. walnuts, finely chopped
1 c. sweetened flaked coconut

In a large bowl, combine butter and sugar; beat until light and fluffy. Add milk and vanilla; beat well. Stir in flour, cherries and walnuts. Shape dough into 7-inch logs. Roll logs in coconut, coating well. Wrap logs in plastic wrap; chill overnight. Unwrap; slice logs into 1/4-inch thick slices. Place on ungreased baking sheets. Bake at 375 degrees for 10 to 12 minutes, until edges are golden. Makes 6 dozen.

Snowball Cookies

Sonya Labbe
West Hollywood, CA

I love making cookies with kids! This recipe is easy enough for them to help. I've liked these cookies since I was a kid myself.

1 c. butter, room temperature
1/4 c. powdered sugar
2 c. all-purpose flour
1/4 t. salt

2 c. sweetened flaked coconut
Garnish: additional powdered
   sugar

In a large bowl, using an electric mixer on medium speed, beat butter with powdered sugar until fluffy. Mix in flour and salt just until combined. Stir in coconut. Roll dough into one-inch balls; place 2 inches apart on ungreased baking sheets. Bake at 350 degrees for 15 to 20 minutes, just until golden. Roll cookies in powdered sugar while still warm; let cool completely. Makes 3 dozen.

Cozy Christmas
COMFORTS

Maple Pecan Icebox Cookies

Sandra Smith
Quartz Hill, CA

These taste like pecan sandies! When Christmas is approaching, I like to make up a dozen or more different kinds of icebox cookies and store them in the refrigerator or freezer. When it gets closer to Christmas, I pull them out and go on a baking marathon!

1 c. butter, room temperature
1/2 c. sugar
1 egg yolk, beaten
2 T. pure maple syrup
1/2 t. vanilla extract
2 c. minus 2 T. all-purpose flour
1-1/4 c. chopped pecans

In a large bowl, beat butter with an electric mixer on medium speed until it whitens and holds soft peaks, 3 to 5 minutes. Beat in sugar until well blended; set aside. In a separate bowl, whisk together egg yolk, maple syrup and vanilla. Beat into butter mixture, mixing just enough to combine. Stir in flour. Fold in pecans; cover and chill until firm. Shape into 4 logs, about 6 inches long; wrap each log in plastic wrap and chill until ready to use. Unwrap; slice logs into 1/4-inch thick slices. Arrange on ungreased baking sheets. Bake at 325 degrees for 12 to 15 minutes, until firm, lightly golden and baked through to the center. Cool on wire racks. Makes 2 to 3 dozen.

Make a neighborly gesture! Deliver a small decorated tree and a plate of cookies to an acquaintance who can't go out easily. Even better, send the kids to do it.

Homemade Cookies & Desserts

Chocolate Chip Shortbread

Kathy Grashoff
Fort Wayne, IN

Scrumptious with a cup of hot coffee or tea! This cookie dough is great to make ahead and tuck in the fridge. Then slice and bake as needed for warm cookies anytime!

1 c. butter, softened
3/4 c. powdered sugar
2 t. vanilla extract
6-oz. pkg. semi-sweet
   chocolate chips

2 c. all-purpose flour
1/4 t. baking powder
1/8 t. salt

In a large bowl, beat butter with an electric mixer on medium speed until creamy. Gradually add powdered sugar, beating until smooth. Stir in vanilla and chocolate chips; set aside. In a separate bowl, stir together remaining ingredients. Gradually add flour mixture to butter mixture, beating on low speed until blended. Shape dough into 3 logs, each 10 inches long. Wrap logs separately in wax paper; chill for 4 hours. Cut each log into 28 slices. Place slices on lightly greased baking sheets, one inch apart. Bake at 350 degrees for 10 to 12 minutes, until edges are golden. Cool on wire racks. Makes 7 dozen.

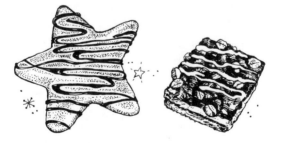

Dress up simple cookies with a yummy chocolate glaze. Combine 1/2 cup chocolate chips with one teaspoon shortening or oil in a microwave-safe bowl. Microwave on high for one minute, stir, then drizzle glaze over cookies. So easy...so pretty!

Cozy Christmas
COMFORTS

Comfort Custard Cake

Janis Parr
Ontario, Canada

This delicious cake is comfort food at its best...spicy, creamy and oh-so-good.

18-1/4 oz. pkg. spice cake mix
3 McIntosh apples, peeled, cored
   and chopped
1 t. vanilla extract
8-oz. container sour cream

14-oz. can sweetened
   condensed milk
1/4 c. lemon juice
1 t. cinnamon

Prepare cake mix according to package directions; stir apples and vanilla into batter. Pour batter into a greased 13"x9" baking pan. Bake at 350 degrees for 35 minutes, or until a toothpick inserted in the center tests done. Meanwhile, in a bowl, combine sour cream and condensed milk; stir in lemon juice. Spread mixture over baked cake while it is hot. Return cake to oven; bake 7 minutes more, or until set. Sprinkle with cinnamon. Serve chilled. Keep any leftovers refrigerated. Serves 12.

Evaporated milk and sweetened condensed milk are both handy in dessert making, but they're not interchangeable. Condensed milk contains sugar and is cooked down to a thickened consistency, while evaporated milk contains no added sugar. Check the label before you bake!

Homemade
Cookies & Desserts

Strawberries in the Snow

Becca Jones
Jackson, TN

For as long as I can remember, my family has been enjoying this wonderful trifle dessert. It is easy to prepare and becomes a favorite of all who try it. I use all low-fat or fat-free products.

16-oz. container strawberries, hulled and sliced
sugar to taste
8-oz. pkg. cream cheese, softened
14-oz. can sweetened condensed milk

1 bakery sour cream angel food cake, sliced or torn into pieces and divided
8-oz. container frozen whipped topping, thawed

In a bowl, combine strawberries and sugar to taste; toss to mix and set aside. In a large bowl, beat cream cheese and condensed milk with an electric mixer on medium speed until smooth. In a clear glass bowl, layer 1/3 each of cake, cream cheese mixture and strawberries. Repeat layers twice; spread with whipped topping. Cover and refrigerate until chilled. Serves 8 to 10.

Chess Squares

Kaye Smith
Jackson, TN

Always a hit with my family & friends! Very easy to make.

18-1/2 oz. pkg. yellow or butter pecan cake mix
4 eggs, room temperature
1/2 c. margarine, room temperature

1 t. vanilla extract
8-oz. pkg. cream cheese, room temperature
16-oz. powdered sugar

Beat together cake mix, one egg, margarine and vanilla. Press evenly into the bottom of a lightly greased 13"x9" glass baking pan; set aside. In a separate bowl, beat together cream cheese and remaining eggs. Slowly add powdered sugar; beat until well mixed. Spoon over crust mixture. Bake at 375 degrees for 30 to 40 minutes, until golden and center feels slightly firm. Cool; cut into squares. Store in an airtight container. Makes 1-1/2 dozen.

Cozy Christmas
COMFORTS

Almond Toffee

*Sharon Welch
LaCygne, KS*

*A wonderful homemade candy! It's best to make this when
it's cool outside like wintertime, otherwise it gets sticky.
The almonds may be omitted, if you prefer.*

1 c. butter
1 c. sugar
3 T. water
1 T. corn syrup

1-1/2 c. chopped almonds
6-oz. pkg. semi-sweet
   chocolate chips

Melt butter in a heavy saucepan over medium heat; gradually stir in sugar. Stir in water and corn syrup. Cook over medium heat, stirring occasionally, until mixture reaches the hard-crack stage, or 290 to 310 degrees on a candy thermometer. Add almonds; cook and stir for another 3 minutes. Spread onto a lightly greased rimmed baking sheet; let cool. Melt chocolate according to package directions; spread over toffee. Cool for several hours; break into pieces. Makes about one pound.

Caramel Cashew Clusters

*Lori Simmons
Princeville, IL*

Yummy! You can also use pecans, peanuts or any favorite nuts.

2 lbs. milk chocolate melting
   chocolate, coarsely chopped
   and divided

1 c. cashew halves
28 caramels, unwrapped
2 T. whipping cream

Line 2 baking sheets with wax paper; butter the paper and set aside. In a microwave-safe bowl, microwave half of chocolate until melted; stir until smooth. Drop chocolate by tablespoonfuls onto baking sheets; let stand about 3 minutes, until partially set. Top each with 6 or 7 cashews. Let stand until completely set. In a heavy saucepan over low heat, combine caramels and cream. Cook and stir until melted and smooth; spoon over cashews. Reheat caramel over low heat if it thickens. Melt remaining chocolate; spoon over caramel and let stand until set. Makes 2-1/2 dozen.

Homemade
Cookies & Desserts

Grandma Louise's Holiday Fruit Balls

Edward Kielar
Whitehouse, OH

Grandma Louise makes these for gifts at holiday time.
When we visit her, she gives everyone a box of these
little confections to enjoy as we drive home.

1-1/2 lbs. candied red cherries,
  chopped
1/2 lb. candied pineapple,
  chopped
8-oz. pkg. chopped dates

7-oz. can sweetened flaked
  coconut
4 c. chopped pecans
14-oz. can sweetened
  condensed milk

Combine cherries, pineapple and dates in a bowl; mix well. Add coconut and pecans. Spoon condensed milk over mixture; stir well. Spoon mixture into paper mini muffin cup liners by teaspoonfuls; set on a baking sheet. Bake at 350 degrees for 20 to 25 minutes. Cool; store in a covered container. May be kept refrigerated for several months. Makes 12 dozen.

Colorful take-out containers are just right for
packing candies and cookies for gift-giving. Tie on
a bow and you're all done!

Cozy Christmas
COMFORTS

Christmas Pie

Jennifer Niemi
Nova Scotia, Canada

With all the flavors of Christmas, this is the perfect dessert for the season...but it's delicious at any time of the year!

1/4 c. all-purpose flour
3/4 c. plus 1 t. sugar, divided
1-1/2 t. cinnamon
1/2 t. ground cloves
1/4 t. nutmeg
1/8 t. salt
2 c. tart apples, peeled, cored and diced
14-oz. can pineapple chunks, drained

3/4 c. raisins
1/2 c. fresh or frozen cranberries
zest of 1 large orange
zest of 1 large lemon
1 T. lemon juice
2 t. rum extract or vanilla extract
2 9-inch pie crusts, unbaked

In a small bowl, combine flour, 3/4 cup sugar, spices and salt; mix well and set aside. In a large bowl, combine fruits, zests, lemon juice and extract. Add flour mixture; mix well. Arrange one pie crust in a 9" pie plate; spoon filling into crust. Top with remaining crust; crimp edges and insert a ceramic pie bird, or cut several vents with a knife tip. Bake at 425 degrees for 15 minutes. Reduce heat to 350 degrees; bake an additional 35 minutes. Sprinkle with remaining sugar immediately after removing from oven. Makes 8 servings.

December is a good time to check out your spice rack. Crush a pinch of each spice...if it has a fresh, zingy scent, it's still good. Toss out any old-smelling spices and stock up on ones you've used up during the year.

Homemade Cookies & Desserts

Gingerbread & Caramel Sauce

Aubrey Nygren
Farmington, NM

This recipe comes from my papa and brings back many wonderful memories from the holidays every time it is made. The recipe calls for only one cup molasses, but for a stronger molasses flavor, add an additional 1/4 cup.

2 eggs, separated	1/2 c. sugar
1 c. molasses	1/2 c. butter, melted
2 t. baking soda	2 c. all-purpose flour
1 t. cinnamon	1 c. boiling water
1 t. ground ginger	Garnish: whipped cream or
1/4 t. nutmeg	ice cream

In a deep bowl, with an electric mixer on high speed, beat egg whites until stiff peaks form; set aside. In a large bowl, mix together molasses, baking soda and spices. Add sugar, butter, egg yolks, flour and boiling water. Mix well; fold in beaten egg whites. Pour batter into a greased 13"x9" baking pan or Bundt® pan. Bake at 350 degrees for 40 minutes, or until a toothpick tests done. At serving time, drizzle individual slices with Caramel Sauce; garnish as desired. Serves 16.

Caramel Sauce:

1 c. boiling water	2 t. all-purpose flour
1 c. brown sugar, packed	1 t. vanilla extract
1/3 c. sugar	1/4 t. nutmeg
1/2 c. butter	1/8 t. salt

Combine all ingredients in a heavy saucepan. Cook over medium heat for 10 to 15 minutes, stirring often.

Live music makes any gathering extra special for guests. Ask a nearby school to recommend a music student who would enjoy playing Christmas carols on piano or violin for you.

Cozy Christmas
COMFORTS

Baked Stuffed Apples

Tamara Mortensen
Iola, WI

This recipe reminds me of a simpler time and makes the house smell so good! It can be kept refrigerated for a few days and reheated to serve. A cozy dessert to share in front of a crackling fireplace!

4 Granny Smith apples
1/3 c. chopped walnuts
1/3 c. sweetened dried cherries
   or cranberries
1/3 c. brown sugar, packed

1-1/2 t. pumpkin pie spice
1/4 c. pure maple syrup
1 T. butter, melted
1/2 c. apple juice
Optional: vanilla ice cream

With an apple corer, scoop out the core and seeds of each apple from the top. Make the opening fairly wide and do not cut through to the bottom. Set aside. In a bowl, mix together walnuts, cherries or cranberries, brown sugar and spice. Stuff apples full of the mixture; arrange in a 9"x9" glass baking pan. Combine maple syrup and butter in a cup; drizzle over apples. Pour apple juice around apples. Cover with aluminum foil; bake at 350 degrees for 40 minutes. Uncover; bake for about 20 minutes longer, until bubbly and very tender. Serve warm, garnished with a scoop of ice cream, if desired. Makes 4 servings.

The crackle of a warm, cozy fire brings everyone together. Enjoy a simple dinner of roasted hot dogs or toasty pie-iron sandwiches and mugs of warm spiced cider in front of the the fireplace. A pan of Baked Stuffed Apples in the oven for dessert will fill the house with a delicious scent.

Homemade Cookies & Desserts

Coconut Macaroons

Cynthia Pagel
Brunswick, MD

This is the only macaroon cookie my family will eat! I found this recipe in an old magazine, and my family expects them during the holidays. They go so quickly, I have to make four batches and hide them in the downstairs refrigerator. Great for gift-giving.

4 egg whites
2/3 c. sugar
1/4 c. all-purpose flour
1/8 t. salt
1/2 t. almond extract

4 c. sweetened flaked coconut
1/4 c. candied red cherries,
  coarsely chopped
1/4 c. candied green cherries,
  coarsely chopped

In a bowl, with an electric mixer on medium speed, beat egg whites until foamy. Add sugar, flour, salt and extract; blend well. Stir in coconut and cherries. Drop by tablespoonfuls onto greased and lightly floured baking sheets, 2 inches apart. Bake at 325 degrees for 13 to 17 minutes, until set and lightly golden. Immediately remove cookies to a wire rack; cool completely. Wrap in wax paper; keep refrigerated. Makes 2 dozen.

Gram's Gingerbread & Pear Cobbler

Sandy Coffey
Cincinnati, OH

My grandma used to make this dessert for holidays...
I have followed it with my own tradition.

1/4 c. butter
1 c. light brown sugar, packed.
3 canned pear halves

14-1/2 oz. pkg. gingerbread mix
Garnish: whipped cream or ice
  cream

In a skillet over medium heat, melt butter with brown sugar; pour into a 1-1/2 quart casserole dish. Carefully arrange pear halves over the mixture, cut-side down; set aside. Prepare gingerbread mix according to package directions; pour batter over pears. Bake at 350 degrees for about one hour, until a toothpick tests done. Cool; turn out onto a platter. Serve warm, garnished as desired. Serves 4 to 6.

Cozy Christmas
COMFORTS

Soft Chocolate Chip Cookies

Billie Jo Elliott
Woodsfield, OH

My granddaughter Cassie loves these chocolate chip cookies. Whenever I make them, I always put some in the freezer for the next time she visits. The pudding mix makes the cookies soft and yummy...you can't stop with just one cookie!

4-1/2 c. all-purpose flour
2 t. baking soda
2 c. butter, softened
1-1/2 c. brown sugar, packed
1/2 c. sugar
2 3.4-oz. pkgs. instant vanilla or
    French vanilla pudding mix

4 eggs, beaten
2 t. vanilla extract
4 c. semi-sweet chocolate chips
Optional: 2 c. chopped walnuts

Sift together flour and baking soda into a bowl; set aside. In a separate large bowl, blend together butter and sugars. Add dry pudding mix; beat until blended. Stir in eggs and vanilla. Blend in flour mixture; fold in chocolate chips and nuts, if using. Drop dough by rounded 1-1/2 tablespoonfuls onto ungreased baking sheets. Bake at 350 degrees for 10 to 12 minutes, until edges are golden. Cool on wire racks. Makes 6 dozen.

Host a caroling party...gather up friends and serenade the neighbors! Back home, have slow cookers full of hot cocoa and spiced cider ready to warm everyone up. Add a platter of cookies and get ready for a merry time together.

Homemade Cookies & Desserts

Best Peanut Butter Cookies

Barb Rudyk
Alberta, Canada

A very easy recipe...you will love these cookies!

1 c. creamy peanut butter
1 c. butter, softened
1 c. sugar
1 c. brown sugar, packed
2 eggs, beaten

1 t. vanilla extract
2-1/2 c. all-purpose flour
1 t. baking powder
1 t. baking soda
1/2 t. salt

In a large bowl, blend peanut butter, butter and sugars. Stir in eggs and vanilla; set aside. In a separate bowl, sift together flour, baking powder, baking soda and salt. Add to peanut butter mixture and mix well. Form dough into balls by rounded teaspoonfuls; place on ungreased baking sheets. Flatten balls slightly; criss-cross with a fork. Bake at 350 degrees for about 12 minutes. Cool on wire racks. Makes 7 dozen.

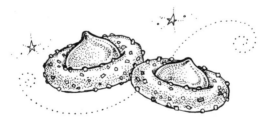

For the quickest bite-size treats, arrange round pretzels on a baking sheet; place a chocolate drop in the center of each. Bake at 350 degrees for for one to 2 minutes. Remove from oven and press a red or green chocolate-coated candy into the center, if desired. Chill until set. Yummy!

Cozy Christmas
COMFORTS

No-Bake Creamy Pumpkin Cheesecake

Wendy Jo Minotte
Duluth, MN

This is a very easy, no-fail pumpkin dessert that's great for the holidays. Best of all, it's a great make-ahead...make it the day before and tuck into the fridge, then just pull it out and serve. You won't be disappointed!

8-oz. pkg. cream cheese,
   softened
1/4 c. butter, softened
1 T. vanilla extract
1/2 t. cinnamon
1/4 t. nutmeg

1/8 t. ground ginger
1/8 t. ground cloves
1-1/2 c. powdered sugar
15-oz. can pumpkin
9-inch graham cracker crust
Garnish: whipped cream

Combine cream cheese, butter, vanilla, spices and powdered sugar in a large bowl. Beat with an electric mixer on medium to high speed for one to 2 minutes, until fluffy. Add pumpkin; beat until well blended. Spoon into pie crust. Cover and chill for 6 hours or overnight. Serve slices topped with whipped cream. Makes 8 servings.

Make your own crumb crusts. Finely crush 1-1/2 cups of graham crackers, vanilla wafers or gingersnaps. Combine with 1/4 cup sugar and 1/2 cup melted butter; press into a pie plate. Chill for 20 minutes or bake at 350 degrees for 10 minutes before adding the filling.

Homemade
Cookies & Desserts

Whipped Eggnog Pie

Jackie Smulski
Lyons, IL

A fluffy, yet richly satisfying cream pie. I like to serve it
on both Christmas and New Year's Day too. Garnish with
a little extra whipped cream and a sprinkle of nutmeg.

3-oz. pkg. cook & serve vanilla
   pudding mix
1-1/2 c. dairy eggnog

1/4 t. nutmeg
2 c. whipping cream
9-inch pie crust, baked

In a saucepan over medium heat, combine dry pudding mix, eggnog
and nutmeg. Cook and stir until mixture comes to a boil. Cook and stir
one to 2 minutes longer, until fully thickened; remove from heat. In a
large deep bowl, beat cream with an electric mixer on high speed until
fluffy. Fold whipped cream into pudding mixture; spoon into pie crust.
Cover and chill. Makes 8 servings.

Triple Layer Chocolate Pie

Becky Holsinger
Belpre, OH

I like to make this easy dessert when I don't have a lot of time
to bake. It always goes quickly at church and family dinners!
I like to garnish the pie with chocolate shavings.

2 3.9-oz. pkgs. instant chocolate
   pudding mix
2 c. cold milk

9-inch chocolate cookie crust
8-oz. container whipped topping,
   thawed and divided

In a large bowl, whisk together dry pudding mixes and milk for
2 minutes, until thickened. Spoon 1-1/2 cups pudding into pie crust.
Stir half of whipped topping into remaining pudding; spread over layer
in crust. Spread with remaining topping. Cover and chill for 3 hours, or
until firm. Serves 6.

Christmas is the family time,
the good time of the year.
– Samuel Johnson

Cozy Christmas
COMFORTS

White Cream Cookies

Marg Friesen
Ontario, Canada

This is our kids' absolute favorite Christmas cookie! I make one batch just for our special day when we as a family of 18 (including ten grandkids!) go out in the bush to find trees for each of our four homes. Later I make another batch for Christmas gatherings. The kids love to make and ice their own!

1 c. sugar
1 c. lard or shortening
1 c. sour cream
1/2 c. milk
2 eggs, beaten
2 t. vanilla extract

3-1/2 c. all-purpose flour
2 T. baking powder
1 t. baking soda
Garnish: colored icing, candy
    sprinkles, crushed peanuts
    or flaked coconut

In a large bowl, combine all ingredients except garnish. Mix well; dough will be very sticky. On a floured surface, roll out dough, 1/4 to 1/2 inch thick. Cut into shapes with cookie cutters. Place on ungreased baking sheets. Bake at 400 degrees for 5 to 8 minutes; cookies will be white when done. Cool cookies on wire racks. Frost and decorate as desired. Makes about 3 dozen.

Cookie cutters make clever napkin rings! Just slip the rolled-up napkin through the center. With a different shape for each person, it's always easy to know whose napkin is whose.

Homemade
Cookies & Desserts

Melting Moments

Beverlee Traxler
British Columbia, Canada

I have made this recipe for a number of years. It was my mom's favorite cookie. She would always say to me, "Bev, these really are melting moments!" and then we would giggle. They really do melt in your mouth!

1 c. butter, softened
3/4 c. powdered sugar
1 t. vanilla extract

1-1/2 c. all-purpose flour
1/2 c. cornstarch
1/4 t. salt

In a large bowl, beat butter and 1/4 cup powdered sugar until creamy. Beat in vanilla; set aside. In a separate bowl, whisk together flour, cornstarch and salt; add to butter mixture and mix well. Cover and refrigerate for one to 2 hours, until firm. Form dough into one-inch balls; place on parchment paper-covered baking sheets, one inch apart. Bake at 350 degrees for 10 to 14 minutes. Cool for 3 to 5 minutes. Transfer to wire racks; sprinkle generously with remaining sugar. Makes 3 dozen.

Kringle Cookies

Janice Woods
Northern Cambria, PA

A favorite cookie to make since my childhood...I now make them with my three daughters. For different occasions, you can change up the color of the sugar used to roll the cookies in.

1 c. butter, softened
1/4 c. sugar
1 t. vanilla extract
2 c. all-purpose flour

1 c. chopped walnuts
Garnish: red and green colored
    sugars

In a large bowl, blend butter and sugar; stir in vanilla. Add flour and nuts; mix well. Shape dough into balls by tablespoonfuls. Roll half the balls in red sugar and the other half in green sugar. Place on greased baking sheets. Bake at 300 degrees for 25 to 30 minutes. Remove immediately to wire racks to cool. Makes 2-1/2 to 3 dozen.

Glazed Pound Cake

Phyllis Roarty
Chesapeake, VA

*I have made this wonderful Bundt® cake for 40 years or more.
In my opinion, it is the best pound cake I have ever tasted! It can
be altered in various ways by changing the flavoring extracts.*

1 c. butter, softened
1/2 c. oil
3 c. sugar
5 eggs
1 t. rum extract or vanilla extract

1 t. coconut extract
3 c. all-purpose flour
1/2 t. baking powder
1/2 t. salt
1 c. milk

In a large bowl, blend butter and oil; add sugar and beat until fluffy.
Add eggs, one at a time, beating for one minute after each egg. Add
extracts; beat well and set aside. In a separate bowl, sift together flour,
baking powder and salt. To butter mixture, add milk alternately with
flour mixture, ending with flour. Pour batter into a greased and floured
Bundt® pan. Bake at 325 degrees for one to 1-1/2 hours, until a
toothpick inserted near the center tests clean. Turn cake out onto a
plate; brush Glaze all over cake. Makes 12 to 15 servings.

Glaze:

1/2 c. sugar
1/4 c. water

1 t. almond extract

Combine all ingredients in a small saucepan. Bring to a boil over
medium heat, stirring well until sugar dissolves.

Grease and flour cake pans in one easy step. Combine 1/4 cup each
of shortening, oil and flour. Store at room temperature in a
covered jar. To use, brush onto cake pan with a pastry brush.

Homemade Cookies & Desserts

German Chocolate Brownies

Rita Brooks
Norman, OK

I've had this recipe for 45 years! I've rarely shared it, but think it's time for everyone else to enjoy these scrumptious brownies.

2 c. self-rising flour	4 sqs. German sweet baking
2 c. sugar	chocolate
4 eggs, beaten	3/4 c. butter

Combine flour, sugar and eggs in a bowl; mix well and set aside. In a saucepan over low heat, melt chocolate with butter; stir well and pour into flour mixture. Stir well until combined. Pour batter into a greased and floured 13"x9" baking pan. Bake at 350 degrees for 30 minutes. Pour Chocolate Icing over brownies. Cool; cut into squares. Makes 16 brownies.

Chocolate Icing:

2 sqs. German sweet baking	1/4 c. butter
chocolate	2 c. powdered sugar

Melt together chocolate and butter in a small saucepan over low heat. Combine with powdered sugar; mix until smooth.

While the family is gathered together, pile everyone in the car for a trip around town to see the Christmas lights and decorations. Sweet memories in the making!

Cozy Christmas
COMFORTS

Pol's Apple Cake

Jeana Owens
Cumberland Gap, TN

I take this cake to church dinners and family reunions...everybody loves it! It is our pastor's favorite cake. I often bake one for him to take home and enjoy. I got this recipe from a telephone bill flyer years ago, and have made this cake often.

3 eggs, beaten
1-1/4 c. oil
2 c. sugar
2-1/2 c. self-rising flour

2 apples, peeled, cored and chopped
1 c. sweetened flaked coconut
1 c. chopped nuts

In a large bowl, blend eggs, oil and sugar until creamy. Add flour a little at a time, mixing well. Fold in apples, coconut and nuts. Spoon batter into a greased and floured tube pan. Bake at 350 degrees for 30 minutes. Remove from oven; set pan on a wire rack and let cool for a full 30 minutes. Turn cake out of pan onto a serving plate; drizzle warm cake with warm Brown Sugar Sauce. Serves 12 to 15.

Brown Sugar Sauce:

1/4 c. butter
1/2 c. brown sugar, packed

1/3 c. evaporated milk

Combine all ingredients in a saucepan over medium-low heat. Boil for 3 minutes, stirring until brown sugar dissolves.

The very name of Christmas,
All that's merry, sweet and gay,
May it bring the very thing
You long for most this happy day.
– From an antique postcard

Homemade
Cookies & Desserts

Shortbread Cookies with Dark Chocolate

Brenda Vanover
Sunland, CA

I used my old faithful shortbread recipe...added a drizzle of dark chocolate and a sprinkle of sea salt to create a "new" cookie. Yum!

1 lb. butter, softened
2 c. powdered sugar
2 t. vanilla extract
4-1/2 c. all-purpose flour

1/2 t. salt
6 sqs. dark baking chocolate, melted
coarse sea salt to taste

In a large bowl, blend together butter, powdered sugar and vanilla. Add flour and salt; mix until blended. Dough will be stiff; if too soft, cover and refrigerate for a few minutes. If desired, dough may be wrapped well and refrigerate up to 2 weeks. At baking time, let dough stand at room temperature until softened enough to roll. Between 2 pieces of parchment paper, roll out dough to 1/4-inch thick, or a little thinner. Cut into desired shapes with cookie cutters. Arrange on parchment paper-lined baking sheets. Bake at 350 degrees for 10 to 12 minutes. Cool on wire racks; drizzle with chocolate and sprinkle with salt as desired. Makes 3 to 4 dozen.

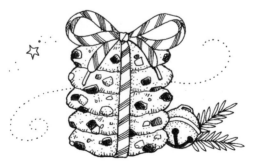

Baking cookies is a terrific activity for first-time cooks. Even the youngest children can help by dropping chocolate chips into the mixing bowl or scooping out spoonfuls of dough. Enjoying the baked cookies will encourage your little helpers to learn more in the kitchen!

Cozy Christmas
COMFORTS

White Christmas Mix

Marsha Baker
Pioneer, OH

I first received a gift of this awesome snack many years ago. Ever since then, it's been a staple in our holiday treats. Pack it into plastic zipping bags and decorate with curly ribbons for a fun and festive gift.

3 c. bite-size crispy rice cereal squares
3 c. bite-size crispy corn cereal squares
3 c. doughnut-shaped oat cereal
2 c. mini pretzels
2 c. salted peanuts
Optional: 10-oz. pkg. red and green candy-coated chocolates
1 lb. white melting chocolate, broken up

In a very large bowl, mix together cereal, pretzels, peanuts and candies, if using. Toss to mix well and set aside. Melt chocolate according to package directions. Pour chocolate over cereal mixture; toss to coat well. Spread on baking sheets; let stand until set. Pack into airtight containers. Makes 14 to 16 cups.

Whip up some snow ice cream...it's creamy and oh-so easy.
With an electric mixer set on high, beat one cup heavy cream
until soft peaks form, then fold in 4 cups freshly fallen snow.
Add sugar and vanilla to taste, and dig in!

Homemade
Cookies & Desserts

Amazing Caramel Corn

Carmen Hyde
Spencerville, IN

This is a tradition in our house. It's a recipe passed on to me by a dear friend years ago. Once you've tasted this caramel corn, you'll never eat prepackaged caramel corn again...ever! Even the kind from the county fair or carnival just doesn't cut it!

24 c. popped corn	1/2 c. light corn syrup
1 c. butter	1/2 t. salt
2 c. brown sugar, packed	1/2 t. baking soda

Place popcorn in a roasting pan or very large bowl; remove any unpopped kernels and set aside. In a heavy saucepan, combine butter, brown sugar, corn syrup and salt. Cook over medium heat, stirring occasionally, until mixture comes to a rolling boil. Cook, stirring constantly, for 5 minutes. Remove from heat; stir in baking soda. Pour hot mixture over popcorn and toss to mix until well coated. Divide popcorn between 2 ungreased rimmed baking sheets. Bake 200 degrees for one hour, gently turning with a pancake turner every 20 minutes. Cool; store in airtight containers. Makes 12 to 16 servings.

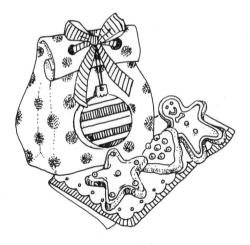

Pack up some homemade treats for a yummy gift. Fill a paper sack, fold down the top, punch 2 holes and insert a colorful ribbon to tie in a bow. Simple!

INDEX

INDEX

Candies

Almond Toffee, 200
Amazing Caramel Corn, 217
Caramel Cashew Clusters, 200
Chocolate Christmas Fudge, 189
Easy Peanut Butter Fudge, 189
White Christmas Mix, 216

Cookies

Best Peanut Butter Cookies, 207
Cherry Pistachio Cookies, 184
Chess Squares, 199
Chocolate Chip Shortbread, 197
Coconut Macaroons, 205
German Chocolate Brownies, 213
Gingerbread Cookies, 193
Gingerbread Crispy Rice Treats, 186
Grandma Letha's Oatmeal Cookies, 192
Grandma Louise's Holiday Fruit
    Balls, 201
Grandma's Frosted Shortbread
    Cookies, 182
Holiday Haystack Cookies, 188
Kringle Cookies, 211
Maple Pecan Icebox Cookies, 196
Melting Moments, 211
Meringue Pecan Bars, 187
Rudolph's Nose Cookies, 194
Santa Claus Whiskers, 195
Shortbread Cookies with Dark
    Chocolate, 215
Snowball Cookies, 195
Soft Chocolate Chip Cookies, 206
Soft Coffee Cookies, 183
Thumbprint Cookies, 185
Vianna's Cinnamon Twists, 186
White Cream Cookies, 210

Desserts

Baked Stuffed Apples, 204
Christmas Pie, 202
Comfort Custard Cake, 198
Cranberry Caramel Cake, 190
Gingerbread & Caramel Sauce, 203
Glazed Pound Cake, 212
Gram's Gingerbread & Pear
    Cobbler, 205
No-Bake Creamy Pumpkin
    Cheesecake, 208
Pol's Apple Cake, 214
Strawberries in the Snow, 199
Triple Layer Chocolate Pie, 209
Warm Winter Lemon Cake, 191
Whipped Eggnog Pie, 209

Mains

Angel Hair Pasta with Tomato &
    Basil, 154
Aunt Barb's Pizza Casserole, 149
Aunt Minnie's Marmalade Pork
    Chops, 167
Balsamic Roast Chicken, 159
Beef & Broccoli Stir-Fry, 162
Best Baked Ziti, 155
Braised Pork Roast with Onion
    Gravy, 166
Chicken & Wild Rice Casserole, 157
Christmas Eve Fish, 153
Company's Coming Chicken, 172
Creamy Pasta Florentine, 154
Easy Turkey Tacos, 146
Eggplant Parmigiana, 171
Grandmama's Chicken & Dressing, 164
Greek Baked Tilapia, 152
Hawaiian Spareribs, 179
Hoppin' John, 180
Mediterranean Party Rice, 168
Mom's Goulash, 156
Nacho Chip Casserole, 147
Nancy's Chicken Delicious, 165
One-Pot Chinese Vegetable
    Casserole, 163
One-Pot Pork Chop Dinner, 173
Pasta Primavera Casserole, 160
Pork Chops in Mushroom & Onion
    Gravy, 151
Salmon au Gratin, 170
Santa Fe Chicken & Rice Casserole, 147
Sausage & Green Bean Dinner, 167
Sausage, Kale & Potato Casserole, 150
Slow-Cooker Beef Tips, 178

219

INDEX

Find Gooseberry Patch
wherever you are!

www.gooseberrypatch.com

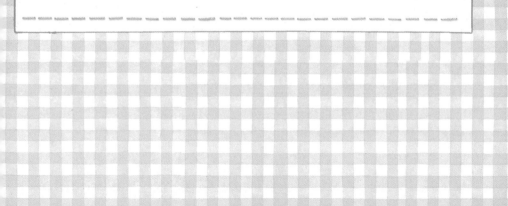

Call us toll-free at 1·800·854·6673

sparkling snowflakes · rosy cheeks

warm gingerbread

chocolatey cocoa

fresh-cut pine

crackling fires

frosty windowpanes · sleigh bells

U.S. to Metric Recipe Equivalents

Volume Measurements

1/4 teaspoon	1 mL
1/2 teaspoon	2 mL
1 teaspoon	5 mL
1 tablespoon = 3 teaspoons	15 mL
2 tablespoons = 1 fluid ounce	30 mL
1/4 cup	60 mL
1/3 cup	75 mL
1/2 cup = 4 fluid ounces	125 mL
1 cup = 8 fluid ounces	250 mL
2 cups = 1 pint =16 fluid ounces	500 mL
4 cups = 1 quart	1 L

Weights

1 ounce	30 g
4 ounces	120 g
8 ounces	225 g
16 ounces = 1 pound	450 g

Oven Temperatures

300° F	150° C
325° F	160° C
350° F	180° C
375° F	190° C
400° F	200° C
450° F	230° C

Baking Pan Sizes

Square

8x8x2 inches	2 L = 20x20x5 cm
9x9x2 inches	2.5 L = 23x23x5 cm

Rectangular

13x9x2 inches	3.5 L = 33x23x5 cm

Loaf

9x5x3 inches	2 L = 23x13x7 cm

Round

8x1-1/2 inches	1.2 L = 20x4 cm
9x1-1/2 inches	1.5 L = 23x4 cm